Growing into Anthroposophy

Four Stages of Spiritual Thinking

Growing into Anthroposophy

Four Stages of Spiritual Thinking

Jan Dostal

Wynstones Press

Published by
Wynstones Press
Ruskin Glass Centre
Wollaston Road
Stourbridge
West Midlands DY8 4HE.
England.

www.wynstonespress.com

First English edition 2011

Translated by Pauline Wehrle
Edited by Matthew Barton

Translated from the original German,
Wie wächst man in die Anthroposophie hinein?
published 1996 by
Verlag Freies Geistesleben GmbH Stuttgart, Germany.

Copyright © original German Verlag Freies Geistesleben 1996.

Copyright © English translation Wynstones Press 2011.
All rights reserved. No part of this publication may be either reproduced or stored by any means whatsoever, including electronic systems, without prior written consent of the copyright holder.

Quotations from the work of Rudolf Steiner have been reproduced with the permission of Rudolf Steiner Press, England.

The right of Jan Dostal to be identified as the author of this work has been asserted by him in accordance with the Design, Copyright and Patents Act 1988.

Cover illustration: *The Bridge* by David Newbatt.

Printed in England.

ISBN 978 0 946206 70 4

Contents

	About the Author	*Page 6*
	Foreword	*Page 7*
One	Prologue: The Stream of Thought Divides	*Page 11*
Two	The First Step: Pure Thinking	*Page 20*
Three	The Second Step: Reverence	*Page 27*
Four	Interlude: The Development of a New Thinking in Rudolf Steiner's Life	*Page 39*
Five	The Third Step: Love	*Page 53*
Six	Interlude: 'Living Thinking'	*Page 75*
Seven	The Fourth Step: Sacrifice	*Page 98*
Eight	Conclusion: Some Consequences	*Page 109*
	Notes and references	*Page 127*

About the Author

Jan Dostal was born into an anthroposophical family in Prague, in 1920. After the second world war in 1945 he became a priest of the Christian Community, but following the ban on the activities of the Christian Community in Czechoslovakia from 1951 onwards, he became a forest worker, then later a music teacher and opera conductor, leading to being the head of a music school. He was the editor of the only pedagogical music magazine, and went on to become chief publisher of the state-owned music publishing house.

In 1977 he had to leave the publishing house because of political reasons and worked as a music school teacher until his retirement. During his life he published a series of pedagogical music works.

Jan Dostal was active in the anthroposophical movement, including during the years of the communist regime when it went underground. Since the fall of communism in 1989 he has contributed to the rebuilding and reconstruction of the anthroposophical society in the new Czech Republic, and especially towards the development of the Czech Steiner Waldorf School movement.

Foreword

I originally intended to publish this booklet without a foreword; but after thorough consideration the publisher said that the booklet absolutely should have one, for readers would wish to know something of the author's motives and intentions.

So be it. Describing how the book came about is no easy matter though, for it is the product of my whole life – which happens to have been rather a long one. The foreword will, I'm afraid, therefore have to contain some aspects of my biography. Is it appropriate to burden readers with things of this sort? I tend to think not! If you wish, you can of course skip it, which I find a comforting thought.

In the Biblical story, an angel stopped Jacob as he was on his way home; to continue on his way, he had to wrestle with him all night. In a somewhat similar way it was my destiny to struggle repeatedly, through a whole lifetime, with the angel of anthroposophy. I was born into an anthroposophical family. The angel of anthroposophy was therefore present in my childhood and I had no problem finding my way into this outlook. I also participated in the life of The Christian Community. I was an intellectual, precocious child, and going to school increased this tendency. The older I grew the more critical I became of everything in my environment, and I also tried to see myself with a critical eye. I became ever more aware of the rift in me between head and heart. My warmth of heart lived in the realm of religion, but my colder intellect not only determined the way I thought about life but also informed my attitude to others. I felt that something in me was not right, but I did not know what I could do to change it.

Later on I tried pursuing the 'path of devotion', and it seemed to make me a little more open-hearted. I also made conscientious efforts to work at the six 'supplementary exercises', and certainly these were of some positive benefit. My previous pleasure in criticizing decreased considerably as time continued. Yet the rift between my thinking and my feeling persisted.

Today, approaching the end of my earthly life, my sense that a rift of this kind can at least be partly healed reminds me of the sentence in Steiner's *Knowledge of the Higher Worlds* that pointed me in the decisive direction: 'The esoteric student has to begin by bringing devotion into his thought life.' I tried to understand what this meant, and repeatedly struggled to make it real in myself. I became aware that I was beginning to think about anthroposophical texts in a different way from before. I could suddenly follow and consciously experience these words in the *Leading Thoughts* which I previously just registered mentally, as though from a distance: 'When he (Michael) enters our intellect it becomes apparent that it is possible for the latter to become an expression of the heart and soul just as much as of the head, the spirit.'

I noticed, too, in my efforts to enter into other people's inner life, that due to today's prevailing culture a great many people suffer from a similar inner rift, even if this phenomenon is expressed in an entirely individual way in each instance. Time and again I observed this in anthroposophists too. My own decades of experience enabled me to understand the great difficulties of putting into practice Rudolf Steiner's constantly repeated emphasis on the need for anthroposophical ideas to enter our feelings and will so that they fertilize and transform our whole inner life. This made me think that if I were to put my own thoughts and experiences down on paper, this might be helpful for others. To start with I wanted to do this in the form of an essay; but this turned into a whole little volume.

Then something else occurred. During these long years in which I tried in vain to build a bridge from the activity of thinking to that of feeling, I also discovered what was for me an unpleasant and even embarrassing split between Steiner's early 'philosophical' writings and his later 'anthroposophical' ones. The 'pure thinking' of his 'philosophical' writings seemed not to accord with the language of his later works. I tried to ignore this fact, but in the long run was unable to. I saw once again just how many of our anthroposophical friends could not cross this bridge either. Having found that a gradual transformation of thinking overcomes this split, it seemed a helpful thing to do to pass on to others my experiences in thinking, however provisional and modest they might be, in the hope these might help others overcome certain difficulties more quickly than I did.

One last thing led to me finally sitting down and starting to write. Family circumstances meant that in the autumn of 1995, contrary to all my intentions, I had to prolong my stay in Germany, which gave me an unusual amount of spare time. I took this as a sign from my destiny to write down the thoughts which had been preoccupying me for years. This is how the book arose.

I hope I have not omitted to mention anything important. There seems to be no further reason why I should hold readers up any longer from getting down to reading the book itself. May it be received with the same reverence and love for anthroposophy with which it has been written.

Jan Dostal

One

Prologue:
The Stream Of Thought Divides

Worldviews that acknowledge life's contradictions in such a profoundly serious way as anthroposophy are few and far between. Religious doctrines tend to ignore contradictory elements, propounding the fundamental oneness of divine existence, while many philosophers try to reconcile all existing contradictions as quickly as possible in a unifying archetypal principle, or two archetypal, metaphysical opposites (such as spirit and matter). In contrast, Rudolf Steiner's consistent endeavour in his works is to fully incorporate into our mental picture of the world the specific nature of life's contradictions. Thus he does not immediately seek to bridge them through general, abstract ideas. In his philosophical writings Steiner demonstrated that he was a convinced advocate of primal world unity as against the many 'duality theories'; yet as he saw it, unity (and we shall speak of this in greater detail in chapter 5) consisted at all levels of an endless plurality, a scarcely fathomable diversity of beings of all kinds and at all levels that are often in blatant opposition to one another. In Steiner's outlook, we do not acquire knowledge in order to haze over or dissolve real contrasts, but, on the contrary, to understand their unmitigated polarity. What a huge array of polarities appear in his worldview; and each time he emphasizes and elucidates them from a different aspect! Light and dark, life and death, hardening and dissolution, sympathy and antipathy, evolution and involution, and every other imaginable contrast are all understood and incorporated as constitutive elements of the world. We are asked to accept the full force of their opposite nature if we wish to arrive at a full grasp of reality. The world is not based on simple, uncontradictory logic. 'Reality is contradictory. We do not understand reality if we do not observe the contradictions that exist in the world.'[1]

Even the thought systems of various worldviews that initially appear incompatible are, according to Steiner, all founded on the world's underlying structure, and mirror the diversity of cosmic inspirations and springs of activity. This is why Steiner emphasizes the equal standing of diverse world conceptions,[2] pointing out that each of them is justified in showing the world in a different light, with divergent core qualities and different laws. Just as a house or a tree offers a different aspect from various perspectives, and only allows us to gain an idea of the whole when all such impressions are harmonized, in the realm of philosophical worldviews the truth is composed of all the different, one-sided angles complementing each other, so that dissonant factors are resolved in an all-encompassing harmony. In this accord the many different aspects find poise and balance.

Such an outlook seems to explain the apparent oddity of the image in one of Paul's epistles to the Ephesians, where truth also emerges as a characteristic of balance: 'Stand therefore, having your loins girt about with truth' (6.14). One may well ask what truth has to do with the loins or hips.[3] The hips, the part of the body with which human beings maintain their pivotal balance in the upright position, have always been connected with the forces of the zodiac sign of the Scales (Libra). Being incorporated into a great, well-poised cosmic harmony – the Scales experience – gives us our bodily support and steadiness in standing upright on the one hand, and on the other gives us the capacity to glimpse the mysterious secret of truth encompassing opposites and offsetting them against each other. Truth does indeed manifest in the sign of the Scales.

Many a contradiction could be clarified and many a cause of bitter dispute avoided if we realized that all phenomena can be approached from different perspectives. The supposed contradictions in Rudolf Steiner's works – to which many of anthroposophy's opponents continually and triumphantly point – can be explained by the fact that Steiner illumines the same subject from different angles, and in doing so allows facts themselves to guide him in characterizing things from divergent points of view.

But one also finds in Steiner's work contradictions of another kind, and these are not connected with his efforts to achieve an all-embracing understanding of the world. Rather they are due to the different ways in which he himself understood and grasped his own spiritual experiences at different periods of his life. When we look at *these* contradictions, it can seem scarcely possible at first glance to reconcile them.

For instance, in the year 1886 Steiner wrote: 'We do not know the world solely in the way it appears to us, but it appears as it is only to our thinking contemplation. *The form of reality that human beings have conceived for themselves in science is the final, true form of it.*'[4]

From the very outset, therefore, this statement seems to conflict with any possibility of a supersensible world!

Compare this with the basic attitude urged by Steiner in his *Occult Science* (1910): 'People who consider "science" to consist solely of what is conveyed to them by means of their senses and the reasoning mind at the service of these, will obviously not accept as science what we are here calling "occult science".' [5]

Or compare the first statement with the next one from the year 1914:

'We have often spoken about what our life of thought, of the senses and of ideas, actually is. I said that fundamentally it is a sort of *mirroring*... And in this way we spend our everyday life entirely within a world of mirror images, with which our own self is interwoven. For we would take hold of our true self only if we could feel ourselves swimming outside our body in spiritual existence.' [6]

The 'final true form of reality' is suddenly dismissed as a mere reflection!

It seems, surely, as if in his younger years Steiner proposed a worldview in which there was scarcely room for a world of spirit, and only later considered it necessary to include outwardly imperceptible realms in his explanation of the world. And, vice versa, in the light of this later worldview, can his earlier view still be given credence?

We can see from Steiner's autobiography that he had clairvoyant experiences from childhood on, and accordingly he himself never doubted the existence of higher realms of existence. So why, in his early philosophical works, including the *Philosophy of Freedom*, doesn't he say a single word about the possible existence of a supersensible world? Or did he originally intend never to say anything at all about his spiritual experiences?

Questions such as these have often been asked. Repeated attempts have been made to find an answer – such as the following: Steiner not only knew very well that there is a supersensible world but also that, in order for our culture to progress in its development, people urgently needed to know about it. At the same time, though, he saw that humankind was not yet mature enough to receive and properly digest such knowledge. He therefore decided to establish a basic framework of knowledge – without for the time being saying anything about worlds of spirit. Building on this, he would only subsequently acquaint people with his findings about higher forms of knowledge such as imagination, inspiration and intuition. This interpretation of a modern initiate's supposed mode of procedure lends the overall impression of a certain noble dignity, in which, for the benefit of humankind, he waited patiently, and only gradually developed in others the understanding they would need to receive his future message when he appeared before the world as a spiritual teacher…

But there is also another, diametrically opposed interpretation of Steiner's contradictory statements at different periods of his work. We could, for instance, posit that Steiner was born as one human being among others, was a child, and did not immediately mature into someone with all-embracing wisdom. He first of all had to work his way through to the level of an initiate – in fact battle his way through to it. And at a particular point in his life he made sincere efforts to outline a worldview based on the thoughts he had so far fully elaborated; and later, at a more mature age, after a long process of clarifying and mentally digesting his thoughts and his spiritual visions he arrived at somewhat different formulations. We should not reproach him, for both he himself and his worldview evolved. Surely we should see him, rather, as a truly inspirational example of a spiritually striving human being. Such an attitude does not try to water down the contradictions in Steiner's work but instead stresses his humanity and his development as a human being – which could actually bring him nearer to the hearts of his readers.

An initiate – a striving human being: wasn't Steiner both of these things? Certainly he was. But not quite in the sense that these two points of view suggest. He was certainly a striving human being who constantly struggled inwardly to evolve to higher stages. But this is no reason to assume that he gradually worked his way upwards from a *materialistic* world conception to a spiritual one – for since childhood he had a natural ability to perceive a supersensible world. This being the case, however, we return to our original question of why, to begin with, he spoke as though what we acquire by means of our senses and our intellect is the whole truth?

The picture of a patient initiate, consistently proceeding according to plan, is not a real one, nor does it correspond with Rudolf Steiner's actual inner development. Even if it purportedly characterizes the life work of a modern initiate, it sounds far too comfortable and problem-free. Just read Steiner's autobiography. You will see that in his third and fourth decade he by no means pre-planned his future career. There is no reason to assume that in the 1880s he saw himself as a future spiritual teacher. Nor could he have published his early writings as a basis for his subsequent teachings. Yet again we face the same question: How are we to explain and understand the contradiction between the world conception in Steiner's earlier writings and all his later work?

This question is the starting point for the present book. My deliberations arise from a conviction that Steiner's philosophical writings are far more than just a philosophical foundation for his spiritual knowledge, but that they represent the first stage of a gigantic struggle to engage with thinking in an entirely new way – a struggle to develop a new, hitherto undiscovered method of forming thoughts capable of *radically transforming modern intellectual thinking into a form of thinking that can grasp the spirit.* A single individual took upon himself the mission of initiating a new kind of thinking for modern and future humanity. A task of this magnitude must surely have required a scarcely conceivable spiritual effort, and taken decades to achieve. The results of these efforts do indeed represent a legacy for all those who choose to concern themselves with Steiner's work – which has not yet received the attention it deserves.

From the account Steiner gives in his autobiography we can take it for granted that, from his early days, his experience of the spirit world was seeking expression in words. But through bitter experience he knew only too well that there was as yet no means of meeting with understanding. Not only was the world a long way from possessing any sort of philosophical basis for findings of this kind, but the whole configuration of modern consciousness – and Steiner, too, had to depend on this form of consciousness in his daily life! – offered no fitting instrument for communicating or receiving them. No soul capacity as yet existed that would enable people to consciously accept or digest such insights, let alone apply them effectively in life. Intellectual, abstract thinking had developed during the previous centuries in a way that was incapable of producing thoughts that could grasp the nature of spirit. Describing this situation later, Steiner said:

'Our powers of cognition are dulled to the spirit. Thinkers are losing the spiritual content in their thoughts. In the idealism of the first half of the nineteenth century they established spiritually empty ideas as though these themselves were the creative content of the world. This is true of Fichte, Schelling and Hegel. Or they pointed to a supersensible element that evaporates because it is void of spirit. Spenser, John Stuart Mill and others were like this. Ideas are dead if they do not seek the living spirit. A spiritual eye for the spirit is fading.'[7]

Even if Steiner did not see himself at all as a future spiritual teacher in the 1880s, it must have seemed to him of vital importance to point to the possibility of experiences which are spiritually alive. But how could this be done? It was essential to find some way to engage with modern thinking devoid of spirit. There was no other soul capacity available for conscious understanding. Steiner was fully aware of the seriousness of the task:

'There arose in me... the need to put my perception of the spiritual world into the form of an account delineated in clear, transparent thoughts. This required an inner withdrawal from everything to which I was connected through external life.'[8]

'An inner withdrawal from everything' meant inwardly letting go of the whole way human beings consciously engaged with the world at that particular time. 'An account delineated in clear, transparent thoughts' would need to arise from an entirely different outlook and from a new perspective. The 'dulled' forces of cognition would have to be strengthened in some way so as to be able to grasp spiritual thoughts. But how was he to do this? Who could have the slightest idea, then, that an historic moment had dawned in human spiritual history? In the 1880s, Steiner made his first great contribution to the further development of modern thinking. And this contribution established the end of the nineteenth century as a turning point of the greatest significance. *The evolving course of human thought, which had developed in the past in markedly different periods – yet each with its own inherent character - divided at that point into two divergent streams moving in different directions.* The one represents a mechanical continuation of previous kinds of thinking, becoming ever more abstract, lifeless and shadowy. It governs humanity's general quest for knowledge and operates at all levels of modern civilization and culture. The other arises imperceptibly and gradually through Steiner's efforts to grasp hold of his spiritual experiences in thought form. The first stage of this process reached its culmination and completion with the publication of the *Philosophy of Freedom* (1893-94).

Two

The First Step: Pure Thinking

We can see from Steiner's autobiography that his efforts to develop spiritually receptive thinking did not initially follow a preconceived plan but always arose – as is true of his later activities – in response to outer promptings. The first such stimulus to give clearer form to his thoughts about the human being and the world was a meeting with Marie Eugenie delle Grazie, a writer whose poetry conveyed a strongly pessimistic, tragic mood, and was filled with a sense of the inevitable triumph over all human ideals of the merciless powers of nature and fate. Steiner felt urged to write to her and suggest the possibility of a different way of looking at life, above all emphasizing a positive view of human freedom. To formulate this he needed to bring his thoughts into a clearer and more focused form: 'This was the moment when the first thoughts began to mature regarding my *Philosophy of Freedom*, which I published later. It was in this letter to delle Grazie that the first seed of this book was conceived.'[9]

This was followed by numerous further promptings of destiny, including a commission to write the introduction to Goethe's scientific writings. Further stimulus came from reading Hamerling's *Homunculus,* study of as yet unpublished manuscripts in the Goethe archive, a conversation with the philosopher Eduard von Hartmann, and conversations with the author Rosa Mayreder. His thoughts for the trajectory of the *Philosophy of*

THE FIRST STEP: PURE THINKING

Freedom were coalescing and growing clearer.

What is the difference between the 'new' thinking which Steiner gradually elaborated at that time, expressed in his philosophical writings at that period, and the outlook we referred to as the general, ongoing stream of intellectual thought? The chief difference was that such thinking was no longer experienced as a generalization of external impressions or their shadowy image, but as an independent and creatively productive spiritual activity: 'The process of cognition now comes to participate actively in the shaping of world reality. By perceiving and knowing this world reality, we become co-creators in it.' [10] Thinking is thus experienced as a real process, as an independent constituent of the world. The same thought is expressed in meditative words in the book *Die Schwelle der geistigen Welt* (The Threshold of the Spiritual World): 'When I think, I experience my unity with the stream of world occurrence.' [11]

As we practise and experience this thinking activity we then become aware that through thinking something is added to the world of our perceptions, which does not itself arise out of this perceived world but comes from a different stratum of existence. These are concepts and interconnected thoughts. Not until this 'something' is added, emerging as though from our inner being, does the reality of things really dawn; for this 'something' contains the secret inherent in things. Only when what manifests in thinking is added to our percepts, are these extended or enhanced to become an actual 'reality', The world of reality is not comprehensible to us, does not have a meaning for us, until we have found thought connections between things and beings (such as cause/effect, younger/older, standing still/moving). The connections thinking reveals to us supply us with the invisible yet real spiritual or mental weft and context[1] for each phenomenon.

But to become aware of all this – of both the active character of thinking and of thoughts' significance for reality – we have to do something apparently straightforward yet extremely unusual: we have to try to observe thinking itself, apply our own thinking to observe our own thinking activity. Our own concepts, ideas and thought connections must become the subject of our study. In his philosophical writings Steiner describes in detail the extent to which we can observe thinking, and how we should set about it. By turning our inner eye to thinking it is possible – perhaps not immediately, but little by little - for us to acknowledge the spiritual reality of the thinking process, the independence of 'thinking in itself' from the process of perceiving. This is Steiner's great discovery.

If we observe our own thinking repeatedly we can come to experience 'pure', 'sense-free' thinking, of which Steiner speaks so often.[12] To many people, of course, an inner activity such as this, unsupported by any sense impressions or sense-based ideas, appears from the start to be barely understandable, and extremely difficult to achieve. But this really is not so. Just try – if possible without resorting to ideas derived from the senses – to think concepts such as 'cause', 'effect', 'wisdom', 'resilience' whilst carefully observing your own thinking; or try to arrive at clear awareness in your own thinking of the relationship between the expressions 'good-better-best', or 'I-you-he/she'; or think about the meaning of insignificant little words such as 'although' or 'in case'. Such exercises can help you slip relatively easily into an experience of non-sensory, purely spiritual meaning. The important thing here is not to try to find other *words* to explain the meaning of these thoughts, but to confine ourselves to allowing the thought content itself – as clearly as can be managed initially – to light up in our consciousness.

Thus what concerned Steiner at the time was to show that by turning thinking in a certain direction we can come to *experience spiritual reality in thinking itself*. In a surprising, new way, therefore, an opportunity was presented whereby people could find confirmation, whenever they wanted, of the existence of the objective reality of the spirit.

If we succeed in entering the realm of sense-free thinking we can notice a subtle but marked difference between thoughts experienced as spiritual reality and ordinary, abstract and shadowy thoughts. The latter usually seem to have little connection with our life of feeling and will. When dealing with ordinary concepts we can certainly examine their authenticity: nothing prevents us from examining whether they are valid or not, true or not. But this kind of examination draws solely on our logical thinking, whereas other, deeper soul forces are not in the least engaged.

Thoughts experienced as reality are quite another matter. They always have a gentle connection with our feeling and will impulses or, to be more precise, with our moral sense. It becomes possible here to experience something similar in the thought realm to what Goethe, in his *Theory of Colours*,[13] says about colours' 'sensory-moral effect'. Sense-free thoughts evoke in us a delicate, otherwise unfamiliar soul resonance; we can experience them as 'morally tinged'. Initially this is just the gentle dawning of such experience; but when we come to describe the second, and particularly the third stage, we will find that this initial level of spiritual thinking can grow and extend. Steiner describes this 'moral colouring' of pure thought in the following way:

'If we want to return again to a spiritual level we really have to make a radical break from everything in the way of mysticism left us from the past, and find the spirit in what one might call a mechanical world now bereft of spirit, which modern science has given us...

'Modern human beings, the people of the civilized world of the end of the 1880s and the beginning of the 1890s for whom I actually wrote my *Philosophy of freedom,* pay attention solely to what can also give rise to constructed technology; they concentrate on the sort of laws governing the physical environment itself. No moral impetus is to be found in that realm, however. Only natural laws can be found or formulated in relation to this domain. As I described it, people in olden times were still connected with their surroundings so that in every stone, plant and animal around them they could still perceive moral impulses, because divine spiritual beings still lived in the whole of nature. These are no longer present in our natural laws. Natural laws contain solely what leads to mechanics and machinery.

'So what was the essential task of this *Philosophy of Freedom*? The essential task was to bring people to realize that, existing as we now do, outside nature, and therefore no longer able to find moral impulses because our senses convey only the laws of nature to us, the only feasible thing is to go out of and beyond ourselves, for we can no longer remain within ourselves. And what I described was the first step towards leaving the physical body. This first step is into pure thinking, as I have described in my *Philosophy of Freedom*. This does not mean sinking into a state of instinctive clairvoyance, but going out of the body altogether, transposing ourselves into the outside world. And what do we have there? By taking the first, tentative step into the beginning of a delicate clairvoyance, we gain moral intuitions; or, to use a more subjective expression, as I did there, "moral imagination". A person detaches from himself in order... to find this spirit in the first place we meet it, in the moral realm.'[14]

When thinking thoughts that are 'pure' or 'sense-free', we experience the world with a moral colouring. To see something in a spiritual way is actually at the same time to see it in a moral way. If we understand the world by means of sense-free thinking, the very nature of these thoughts will invoke a moral response. The intuitions from which pure thinking draws its content are at the same time morally inspired intuitions. In experiencing truth as spiritual reality, people at the same time experience its connection with the realm of moral ideas, the realm of what is good. In this connection, Steiner characterized his intentions as follows:

'In this field I was at that time less concerned about presenting the spiritual world as such, in which human beings experience their moral intuitions, preferring instead to emphasize the spiritual character of these intuitions themselves.'[15]

This was therefore the *first step* in Steiner's efforts to transform outmoded brain thinking into an organ for experiencing the spirit. He drew attention to sense-free thinking as something that can light up in our life of soul as a spiritual fact. In this kind of thinking we can already experience the existence of a coherent supersensible world. Without as yet being intellectually conscious of his future activity as a spiritual teacher, nor even wanting as yet to plan for such a future, but purely in struggling to make it possible for people to grasp their spiritual dimension, Steiner created a reliable epistemological basis both for his later teaching and for a conscious reception of spiritual findings.

In looking back on his philosophical works of that period, he was therefore able to say:

'These works stand at a very significant intermediary stage between knowledge of the sense world and knowledge of the spiritual world. They offer what thinking can acquire when it raises itself above sense observation but does not yet embark on spiritual research. Anyone who allows these writings to work on his whole soul is already in the spiritual world, though conveyed to him still as a thought world. Those who feel able to allow an intermediary stage of this kind to work on them are on a reliable path upon which they can acquire the sort of feeling for the higher world which will be most fruitful for them throughout their future existence.' [16]

Thus we become aware of the spiritual world in thinking. In the much-quoted words from his introduction to the second volume of Goethe's scientific writing, Steiner put it like this:

'When thinking grasps hold of an idea, it fuses with the originating foundation of world existence. What is at work externally enters the human spirit so that we become *one* with objective reality to the highest degree. *Becoming aware how the idea lives in reality is true human communion.*'

Three

The Second Step: Reverence

Steiner patiently and persistently related all his work and activities to modern intellectual thinking. This, of course, is true particularly of his philosophical works. They can be understood purely by means of this thinking insofar as, in following Steiner's explanations, one is prepared to carry out the described shift – that is, withdrawing from perceived things and the mental images of them and attending to one's own thinking activity. By this means even the most intellectual thinking can, at the level of sense-free concepts, experience a spiritual world.

Having achieved this, however, does not yet enable one to consciously grasp in thinking the inner content of what Steiner refers to, from the turn of the century onwards, as imagination, inspiration and intuition. We can delude ourselves about this in various ways. But if we face up fairly and squarely to our own capacity for understanding, we can discover the truth of this. What hinders us from grasping such spiritual content is the general inability of our intellect to comprehend something that is of a considerably higher nature than we ourselves. Our thinking capacity can grasp the mineral world, and to some extent also the conditions pertaining to plant and animal realms, and human life; but we lack the necessary prerequisite of personal experience to comprehend an angel or an archangel not only as an abstract concept but also in their essential nature.

As we cannot, ourselves, perceive them, we cannot find thought intuitions suited to consciously understanding them. Many people are aware of this inability, which is why, on principle, they put aside books about higher worlds. They do not want to be dishonest with themselves, or pretend they understand what they are reading – which after all is bound to be mere words to them.

Is there any way at all, then, in which thinking can approach circumstances or beings that are beyond or above us? From whichever point of view we try to approach this question we shall find at each point that there is only one key to the door of higher knowledge: a feeling of *reverence*. If I can imbue my concept of an angel with a corresponding degree of reverence, nothing hinders me any more from understanding its clearly superior nature. 'Pupils of esotericism have to start', says Steiner, 'by incorporating devotion into their life of thinking'.[17] This does *not* mean merely having reverent feelings *alongside* thinking; the essential thing is that these feelings penetrate our thinking itself. If I am to think an angelic being I have to be able to allow my own sense of this being's ethical elevation, compared to me, to light up in my thoughts. And the higher the being I want to understand, the deeper the reverence must be with which I receive it into my thoughts. To study any work of spiritual science, our thoughts have to be warmed by particular feelings, especially feelings of admiration, veneration, and humility; only then can we be properly receptive to accounts of divine, spiritual beings. This law applies to anything we seek to learn in the realm of supersensible knowledge.

This also helps us understand what Steiner means when he stated in the preface to *Theosophy* (1904):

'This book cannot be read in the way we usually read books nowadays. In a certain respect every page, in fact every sentence, has to be *worked at*. It requires conscious struggle. This is the only way to enable the book to mean for you what it ought to mean. If you merely read through it, you will not have read it at all. Its truths have to be *experienced*. It is only in this sense that spiritual science has any value.' [18]

Do we take such promptings seriously? Do we give them their proper due in anthroposophical work? Do we try to work our way into texts in this way? What does it really mean 'to work at something'? Is this simply to do with pondering over a paragraph until the logical connections become clearer? No, it surely means much more than that. We have to make an effort not only to engage our thinking but also to include deeper soul activities in our study; for not until we inform our endeavours with feelings of self-detachment and reverence will we be capable of '*experiencing* the truths of such a book' in the way Steiner asks us to. He is emphatically clear, indeed, that 'it is only in this sense that spiritual science has any value'.

In the fourth section of the first chapter of *Theosophy*, Steiner again comes to speak about mental work accompanied by feelings, but this time from a somewhat different point of view: 'Our most sublime feelings are certainly not those that "arise of themselves", but those that are achieved by energetic and persevering work in the realm of thought.' Esoteric pupils should be living in such feelings as they study, he suggests, for these render their thinking receptive to higher realities.

While Steiner was working within the Theosophical Society we find only brief remarks in his works about such cooperation between head and heart. However, he deals with this theme in a far-reaching and fundamental way in the lecture cycle *The World of the Senses and the World of the Spirit*,[19] where wonder and reverence are described as the prerequisite for, and initial stages of all real knowledge of the world. Strange to say, he does not speak about this again in such detail in any other of his numerous lectures.

Why is this? Evidently it was because his anthroposophical work faced him with another problem connected with the fundamental need to develop clarity in thinking itself. At that period Steiner repeatedly highlighted the importance of logical thinking, emphasizing time and again its task in human evolution. We can sense how hard he was working to awaken a modern type of consciousness in the devoted, religiously-minded older members of the Theosophical Society. On the other hand, we can take it for granted that when the capacity to think stirred into greater activity in these members of the Theosophical Society, then their abundant feelings of devotion will have united as though by themselves with the mental work they were doing in studying spiritual-scientific findings. Steiner must therefore have had little reason at the time to choose that particular theme for further elaboration.

Admittedly, he repeatedly refers in his lectures to the need for a thinking impregnated with feeling; but these are only isolated statements, which appear to take for granted that his audience have already encountered the subject, or perhaps are so receptive that they can receive what they hear immediately.[20]

However, years later, in the very last period of his work, and from a very different perspective, Steiner returns to the cooperative work of head and heart in connection with the Michael mystery. He describes how 'cosmic intelligence' was originally administered by the archangel Michael, but in modern times was entrusted to humankind itself. As human beings now live in the age of freedom and it is up to them how they will use this intelligence, the question arises for the angelic beings above them whether the original, divine intelligence will now fall prey, in the form of cold, apathetic intellect, to the ahrimanic sphere, or whether it will find its way back to super-personal love in the sphere of Christ and Michael:

'That was the great crisis – which we are still in the midst of, and that comes to expression as Ahriman's battle with Michael. For Ahriman is using all his power to challenge Michael's rulership over intelligence that has now become earthly; and Michael, with all the impulses that are his, though his dominion over intelligence has lapsed from him, is striving to take hold of it again at the beginning of his new earthly rule, from the year 1879 onwards.' [21]

The outcome is up to human beings. And the decisive way in which Ahriman-related and Michael-related intellectuality are different lies in the fact that ahrimanized intellectuality is solely head intelligence, whereas the Michael kind involves participation of the whole human being:

'Intellectuality streams out from Ahriman as an ice-cold, soulless cosmic impulse, and those caught in the grip of this acquire the sort of logic that appears to speak for itself in a loveless, merciless way, whereas in truth it is Ahriman speaking within it; and it shows no trace of the real, inner connectedness apparent in someone in whom heart and soul imbue what they think, say or do.

'... When Michael fills our intelligence, the possibility is there for our words to be just as much an expression of the heart

– the soul, as of the head – the spirit. For Michael possesses the originating, creative forces both of the gods and also of human beings. Therefore he brings to intelligence nothing of an icy coldness or soullessness, but on the contrary accompanies it with a deep inner warmth.' [22]

'The Age of Michael has dawned. Hearts are beginning to have thoughts; enthusiasm comes no longer merely from the shadowy realm of mysticism but from souls uplifted by the clarity of thoughts. To understand this means to take Michael into the spiritual aspirations of our hearts. Thoughts, which today have leanings towards the spirit, must arise from hearts that beat for Michael, the fiery thought-prince of the cosmos.' [23]

When heart forces are engaged in our thinking processes, knowledge of the divine-spiritual world can spring to life in human thinking as we have described, and intelligence, illumined by the spirit, can stream towards Michael in a new way. This new approach to thinking is *the second stage of the transformation of our human ability to think.*

But let us go further and ask what happens when particular feelings are included in the concept-forming process. Can we characterize this newly acquired change more precisely?

Certainly we can. Firstly, human beings no longer approach knowledge as usurpers who automatically assume the right to seize hold of any kind of knowledge whenever they like. Concepts, conclusions and judgements are no longer considered to be tongs or forceps used ruthlessly to extract items of knowledge. Instead, concepts become vessels raised as an invitation to receive a response as a gift of grace. We do not *seize hold* of knowledge any longer but inwardly *entreat* for it: a radical change in our attitude to the acquisition of knowledge.

The second difference concerns the character and form of concepts themselves. In ordinary thinking we usually try to shape our concepts as unambiguously, clearly and unalterably as possible. We see this as a requirement of a thinking that exactly corresponds to its subject. Every concept should be clearly defined, and distinct and separate from all others. If you construct a picture of the world with concepts of this kind it will appear to be made of nothing but entirely separate bricks. The world will then necessarily be thought of as discontinuous – as though fitted together out of individual molecules or atoms, for instance - whereas all such ideas are nothing more than a mirror image of the discontinuous thinking that formed them. Thinking tries, first, to cut the world up into pieces, in order to be able to understand it; for, after all, it cannot picture the world in any other way than as consisting of single, disconnected parts.

The spiritual world knows nothing of such neat divisions of its constituent parts. It is worth recalling the description of 'spirit land' in *Theosophy*:

'For the archetypes are *creative beings*. They are the master builders of all that comes into being in the physical world and the soul world. Their forms change rapidly, and in each archetype there is the possibility of assuming myriad specialized forms. They let the different forms spring forth, as it were, from themselves; and no sooner is one produced than the archetype sets about pouring forth the next. The archetypes stand in a more or less close relationship to each other. They do not work singly. One requires the help of another in their creations. Innumerable archetypes often cooperate so that one or another being in the soul world or the physical world may arise.'

If we are really honest with ourselves we have to realize that our ordinary thinking must capitulate here. When we are presented with something of this kind we cannot grasp it in our discontinuous concepts. And this will be the case until thinking becomes imbued with impulses of feeling. Everyone knows that feelings themselves are not so sharply outlined, fixed and separate from other things as ordinary concepts are, nor can they be brought into a clear, logically constructed system. Every kind of feeling can assume innumerable nuances, and express itself in innumerable transitions to other feelings. If we call a feeling 'wonder' or 'reverence', it is only a fairly vague reference to a wide and colourful area of inner experience, and we must remain aware of the fact that no definite limits exist between feelings described in that way.

When thinking is enlivened by feeling it acquires mobility and the ability to transform, developing the capacity to create seamless transitions to other concepts. The world no longer has to be visualized in terms of separate cosmic bricks, but can instead be grasped as a single, harmonious stream comprehending everything. In principle, we then arrive at the possibility of grasping in thought the interwoven life of the world of spirit.

But there is one thing we must not forget here. The concepts that have now come into movement should not for this reason lose their clarity, their uniqueness. To think these concepts clearly at this stage is certainly more demanding than before. But one has to keep one's eye on the fact that the world, in reality, is by no means a box of bricks, and that if you think in terms of the all-too-easy 'box-of-bricks' paradigm you can at most piece together a subjectively satisfying, hypothetical structure, but not a world picture that is true to reality. It was not by chance that in his lecture on 'Practical Training in Thought'[24] Steiner immediately suggests to his pupils, in the very first thinking exercise he sets them, the task of forming concepts of forms and colours in a process of change: one day after another, at a set time, the pupils should observe the moving clouds, and compare those of one day to those of the previous day; mere head logic would be bound to fail in this. Moving clouds are doubtless a distinct phenomenon, but our thinking ability has first to work its way through to this kind of mobile clarity.

As stated in the *Philosophy of Freedom*, each percept has its corresponding concept, found by means of what Steiner calls 'intuition.' Something similar obviously applies to the forming of spiritual-scientific concepts at this stage. Now, however, one does not proceed from one's own percepts or mental images but from thoughts contained in a spiritual-scientific book. To understand these, here too we have to add the corresponding intuitions. This means that we need to inwardly form concepts *tinged by the right feeling nuances, and corresponding to the particular content*. The reverence actively participating in this process will assume varying levels of intensity and tinges of feeling, for every spiritual-scientific picture or thought requires a specific shade of feeling intensity. Our conscious engagement with a spiritual-scientific text will also always depend on the extent to which we find the right intuitions in which head and heart cooperate, and how clearly this enables us to understand the content.

To bring home to us what is actually meant by this, let me venture to suggest something – even if only in schematic outline. If a spiritual-scientific text speaks about elemental beings, let us say, or similar phenomena in the realm of nature spirits, we can try to properly grasp them with our thinking by imbuing it with the subtlest nuance of reverential feeling, a tinge of what we generally call 'admiration'; whereas, if angels or archangels are the subject of discussion – in other words, beings clearly ranked higher than ourselves - we will need to accompany our reading with a somewhat deeper reverence: that is, with true reverence itself. If, on the other hand, we are not only taking note, more or less, of the outward appearance of cosmic beings of the higher order – say, cherubim or seraphim – but are making way for them to stream into our thinking about the world in a 'real' way, we also have to lift the degree of reverence active in our thinking to the highest level of enthusiasm, for otherwise the significance of such concepts escapes us. In relation to every being or phenomenon, therefore, our intuitions have to supply us with a different, corresponding kind of feeling-imbued concept.

This level of thinking should not of course be limited to spiritual-scientific communications. Nothing prevents us from meeting the visible world, too, with the same thinking approach, if we want to. The reverence streaming into our thinking will then allow us to become aware in the kingdoms of nature ranged apparently 'beneath us', of impressions inaccessible to our sense experience – impressions that come from life forces, and from the sphere of soul and spirit. In the human realm, too, many a new understanding can open up to us, if we are prepared to approach another person with reverence for their inmost being, and make an effort to understand their intentions and will. Only by striving for such inner openness in the face of what is, initially, something remote from, or foreign to us, can we establish real social cohesion.

Reverence also however triggers a further important quality in the realm of thinking itself; this new kind of thinking, as we discover, enables us to enter a quite different logical domain. Feelings of admiration or reverence repeatedly reveal the untenable nature of normal intellectual reflection, of a logic in other words that is lifeless in contrast with living phenomena. Take Darwin's theory of evolution, for instance, which posits that innumerable, small but inherited chance modifications of the bodily forms of organisms gradually attain increasing perfection. Living creatures with more perfect organs compared with those of less perfect creatures – that remain at a previous stage of development – are thought to hold their own more easily in the struggle for existence, and thus to propagate the achieved 'improvements'. This theory did not originate behind a desk. It is based on a great number of single observations and can appear logical and convincing to ordinary thinking. However, this applies only so long as we do not, in our thinking, call on the help of admiration or wonder. Try, with the aid of natural wonder, to look at any single part of an animal or insect body. Look, for example, at the way a garden spider makes its elaborate web. It does so by using its spinning gland to excrete a fluid, which is squeezed out of its body through spinnerets and, in the air, immediately clots into a thin thread. On the spiders' feet there is, in addition, a special device with the help of which the various threads are pulled in different directions and form themselves into a web. As soon as you have really felt the miracle of this bodily organism, you know *without any further proof,* that the logic of 'small chance modifications' cannot possibly be correct. You will know, by direct evidence, and with full clarity, that any picture of evolution running on more or less mechanical lines is untenable – even if, by means of ordinary logic, it is very difficult to explain the incorrectness of such a theory of evolution.

On the other hand, by drawing the feeling we have been talking about into the process of understanding, we can really grasp the wisdom-filled inner logic of many spiritual-scientific accounts, which, looked at superficially, appear at first to be illogical. The logic you discover in these texts is not of the sort that connects one judgement with another in a linear way, but is related instead to artistic forms. With the help of the kind of thinking imbued with reverence, we recognize ever more clearly that the world is not a mechanism, not a cosmic machine, but a divine work of art.

Ordinary contemporary habits of thought often make it difficult, even for those who are open to the spirit, to imagine that understanding the world, or understanding anthroposophy relies decisively on gently imbuing thoughts with feelings. In this context we can recall words by Steiner:

'It is not easy initially to believe that feelings such as reverence, respect and so on have anything to do with cognition. This is because we are inclined to set cognition aside as a faculty by itself – one that stands in no relation to what otherwise transpires in the soul. In thinking like this we overlook the fact that the soul exercises the cognitive faculty; and feelings are for the soul what food is for the body. If we give the body stones in place of bread its activity will cease. It is the same with the soul. Veneration, respect and devotion are nourishment that render it healthy and strong; and strong, especially, for the activity of cognition. Disrespect, antipathy, under-estimation of what deserves recognition, on the other hand, exert a paralyzing and withering effect on this cognitive faculty.' [25]

Four

Interlude: The Development of a New Thinking in Rudolf Steiner's Life

Both the first and second stages of spiritual thinking can only be achieved by taking a radical step, in each instance, in a new, previously unknown direction. The 'pure thinking' of Rudolf Steiner's philosophical writings differs deeply from ordinary thinking in that it alters the direction of our focus to look at the activity of thinking itself. There is a clear gulf between ordinary thinking and the kind to be newly acquired, and this has to be bridged. If we succeed in doing this then we acquire an entirely new relationship to the world. As long as we think intellectually we remain caught up in the sense world. To practise the 'pure thinking' experience – thus taking a step on the path to higher knowledge, whether we do so intentionally or not – is to enter into a personal relationship with the spiritual world.

But likewise there is a gulf, bridged by inner development, marking the transition between the first and the second steps – the stage of reverence, at which we open our thinking to the spirit. By taking this further step we acquire the capacity to absorb spiritual facts and beings into our thinking in a fitting way.

If we think of this double step, it appears comprehensible that in Rudolf Steiner's own work the two stages did not occur at one and the same time, but one after the other, during long years of effort: that he achieved the first step – grasping the spirit through thought – in the last two decades of the nineteenth century, largely in a period in which he had not yet (or at least not clearly) visualized his goal of working as a spiritual teacher. Not until the beginning of the new century, when destiny set him the task of speaking openly about higher worlds, did he concern himself more thoroughly with the nature of a thinking capable also of receiving spiritual realities. We see the fruits of these efforts in the works he produced while active in the Theosophical Society.

If we really make clear to ourselves that this second kind of thinking activity was what first opened up to those who were neither initiated nor clairvoyant hitherto unsuspected possibilities of finding their way into higher truths, then we will fully grasp many a contradiction that is to be found in comments by Steiner before and after the turn of the century.

What was he aiming for before the end of the century? He wished to grasp the actual spirit in thinking itself. In his works of that period he did not yet speak of higher worlds but exclusively and repeatedly of the unique quality of thinking and its significance for understanding the world. Rudolf Steiner spoke to his readers' hearts when he said: You perceive the world with your senses. What you perceive in this way is only part of reality, which in itself inevitably remains incomprehensible. But by enlisting the help of thinking, and complementing what you perceive with the content of your thinking, you can discover that your own thinking enables you to grasp the true essence of things. And by uniting these two, perception and thinking, you can access the true nature of things. You do not require anything more than this to understand the world. There is no need therefore to look for anything beyond sense perception and thinking.

INTERLUDE: THE DEVELOPMENT OF A NEW THINKING 41

Steiner presents this thought time and again, in many variations, as the core idea of his theory of knowedge. For instance:[26]

'As citizens of two worlds, the world of the senses and the world of the spirit, the one coming towards us from below, the other shining in from above, we grasp scientific knowledge by combining the two in one undivided unity. Outer form calls for our attention from the one direction, and inner being calls from the other; we have to unite the two.

'Our work has shown us that any assumption of a form of existence lying outside ideas is an absurdity. The entire foundations of existence have been poured out into the world and have merged with it. In our thinking we see it in its most perfect form, as it is in itself.

'The form of reality that human beings have conceived for themselves in science is the final, true form of it.'

Steiner says the same thing later on, too, when looking back on his views at the time:

'Perceiving with their senses, human beings see the world as an illusion. When however, sense-free thinking joins, within us, with sense perception, the illusion is imbued with reality and ceases to be an illusion. The human spirit, experiencing itself within, meets the spirit of the world, which now is not *hidden behind the sense world, but lives and moves within it.*' [27]

'The precondition for knowledge to arise is therefore *through* and *for* the "I". It is the latter itself that asks cognitive questions. In fact it derives them from the absolutely clear, inherently transparent element of thinking. If we ask a question we ourselves cannot answer, the content of the question itself, in all its ramifications, cannot be entirely clear. The world does not pose us questions, but we ourselves pose them.'[28]

I believe we can readily understand how keen Steiner was to keep emphatically urging the following on his readers: Do not persist in visualizing spirit as something mysteriously hazy, inaccessible, unreachable. You do not have to look for it in a distant, unapproachable realm of dreams, beyond space and time, because you can experience it in the world you know, within the world given you through sense perception and your own thinking activity, if only you properly grasp the nature of thinking. The spirit of the world can manifest directly in your thinking. You have access, through thinking, to the 'things in themselves'.

At that time there was, of course, a chasm between the way Steiner himself experienced the world and the way his readers were able to experience it. From childhood on, Steiner had been able to perceive supersensibly; we can see from his autobiography that in the decades we have been considering he had spiritual insights into specific examples of reincarnation and karma.[29] In those days already, therefore, the expression 'spirit of the world' had a clearer, incomparably richer content for him than the readers of his philosophical books could have possibly imagined. He was already taking great care when formulating his views, that, in his choice of wording he was saying nothing – even if unnoticed by others – that would contradict his spiritual experiences. What he expressed in his books had the same significance for him as his experiences in supersensible regions. He put this in words by saying:

'The way the sense world appears to human perception is not a reality. It is real when combined with what is revealed to human beings in thought... The same is true of spiritual perception. When this occurs through soul processes I have described in my later book *Knowledge of the Higher Worlds,* it again presents us with *one* aspect of – spiritual – reality, while corresponding thoughts about the spirit present the other.'[30]

What Steiner was explaining in epistemological terms applies, then, both to life in physical, sensory reality and to life in the spiritual world. That is how Steiner understood it on his own behalf.

His readers, of course, could not know anything about the relationship Steiner already had at that time to a supersensible world. To judge by Steiner's books, his readers were fully entitled to presume that the world accessible to their own senses was the only real one, and that the 'spirit' manifests in human beings solely in the form of thoughts about the sense world. So it could well have come to them as a shock, as contradictory to the contents of his previous books, to read later on in *Occult Science*:

'The whole of occult science must germinate from two thoughts, which can take root in every human being... These two thoughts are, that firstly behind the physical world there exists an invisible world, *concealed to begin with* from the senses, and from thinking bound up with the senses; and secondly that it is possible, by developing capacities slumbering within us, for human beings to penetrate this hidden world.'

Suddenly Steiner raises questions which the world confronts us with, and which we cannot answer with our thinking:

'We can become clear about the fact that when we observe the visible world it presents us with problems which can never be solved through the intrinsic facts of this world itself... For, through their own inner nature, the visible facts point clearly to a hidden world. Those who do not realize this close their minds to the riddles that spring up everywhere from the sense world's facts. They *refuse* to perceive certain questions and problems, therefore they believe that all problems can be solved by means of the obvious facts.'[31]

All of a sudden the reader is told of an invisible world hidden *behind* the visible one; a visible world which presents human beings with questions and riddles that cannot be solved through this world's own inherent realities. He hears of dormant faculties that are not yet manifest, but which have to be developed! Can we imagine a more blatant contrast to the epistemological convictions previously expressed? It would nevertheless be quite wrong to present the two views as irreconcilably opposed. This would be the same as describing a particular landscape you see at one moment when out for a walk, and then, later on, looking at the landscape and requiring, for the sake of uniformity, that it should be identical to your previous impression. Or observing a plant in its sprouting state, before the bud opens, and then in full bloom, and insisting that the second form should be identical with the first. The identity of the two forms is not in their resemblance to each other but solely in the process of development they share in pursuing their original growth impulse.

Steiner's philosophical books and his spiritual scientific works were written at different periods of his activity, and therefore draw readers' attention in different directions. It would be wrong to conclude from this that in the interval between them Steiner had altered his inner stance. On the contrary: his basic philosophical principles fully underpin his later spiritual revelations, and vice versa. It was just that in the two different periods he had different things to report and was also to some extent addressing a different readership.

In the first period he drew attention to the fact that already in the sense world itself our thinking can acknowledge the existence of a coherent world of mind or spirit. His later writings did not alter this conclusion. The world of thoughts is a valid expression of the spiritual world, and the reality of this spirit world can indeed be experienced in the forming of thoughts. It is just that the concept 'reality' can be thought at various levels of intensity, and can also undergo transformations in us. Pure thoughts form the lowest, most shadowy of these levels. If we then start to sense that there are higher stages of reality, questions arise that previously we had no reason to ask. *Behind* (or *above*) the world previously experienced as reality we can now start looking for a higher cosmic reality. An important aspect in this regard is that although this cosmic reality is as yet only guessed at and not perceived, in principle it does not have to remain imperceptible. In the course of higher development, with the unfolding of capacities which hitherto only existed in seed form, human beings will become able to experience higher levels of reality, though once again these need to be supplemented by a – now more highly developed – thinking, to endow them with full reality.

Thus, in the second period of his activity, Steiner's destiny led him by gradual stages to open up for his fellow human beings the vast universe of higher spirit reality: realms of divine, spiritual existence that rank high above generally accessible levels of reality but which, nevertheless, are invisibly and creatively at work in the sense world, bringing it to life and developing it. As far as our present level of consciousness is concerned, therefore, these realms are 'behind' the sense world, yet they are at the same time to be looked for 'in' it. And Steiner was of course expecting his readers to engage with these findings, with the help of a transformed, more highly developed thinking.

It is this other kind of thinking – which we have called the second level of thinking's transformation – which Steiner addresses in his spiritual scientific books. *His writing style also becomes essentially different.* Above all, his readers find that Steiner's texts suddenly become much more 'difficult' to understand. Why is this?

As before, Steiner addresses contemporary intellectual thinking with extreme patience initially; that is, he starts with familiar concepts, and tries not to affront intellectual logic too much. This forms as it were the lowest level of his presentations. But this level is just an outward support. In his philosophical works, starting from this level, he endeavours to lead his readers to the next level, to 'pure thinking'. To follow him in this, all that his readers needed was a logical kind of thinking. There was no reason to fetch into their thinking any impulses from deeper soul levels. Put bluntly, people could understand the *Philosophy of Freedom* whether they were rich or poor in feeling, pious or godless, moral or immoral. They had only to be capable of 'thinking about their thinking', of making it an object of inner observation. The form (but not the content!) of these writings mostly accorded with normal trains of thought, which made them considerably easier to understand. The style hardly differed at all from the style used in other popular, contemporary philosophical writings. This may very likely have been due in part to his earlier editorial experience.

In his spiritual scientific works, however, Steiner adopts a different mode of expression. He makes concessions to his readers by descending to the intellectual plane. But now he expects his readers, without any special mention of observation of thinking, to raise themselves to the plane of 'pure thinking.' For pure thinking, the kind that perceives itself, is after all a prerequisite for engaging with the second level, that of 'Michaelic' thinking – thinking infused with feeling. The apparent 'difficulty' of Steiner's new style is caused by the fact that he now 'consciously endeavours' to draw the readers' attention again and again to their own thoughts: they must, so to speak, continually account to themselves for the way they formulate their thoughts. Where readers attempt to pursue ordinary paths of thought, they are often suddenly mercilessly torn away from these and must try, once again, to understand by paying closer attention to the direction or motion of their thinking. This constant renewal of awareness of their own thinking is perpetually present in these works as a quiet undertone; and the fact that their subject matter is mostly of a supersensible nature makes it easier to develop 'sense-free' thinking.

In *Occult Science,* Steiner highlights the fact that active participation in reading a text already helps to transpose readers into spiritual reality; that reading can – and really ought to – take place in such a way that the very manner in which they form thoughts will allow them to experience 'the stream of spiritual existence':

'The reader of communications about spiritual scientific knowledge undergoes experiences in a quite different way from the reader of communications about external facts. When we read of the outer sense world we are *reading about* them.

But when we read of supersensible facts in the right way, we are *living in* the stream of spiritual existence. When we absorb the results of supersensible investigation we enter, at the same time, upon our own inner path towards them. It is true that readers often do not observe what is meant here. Entering the spiritual world is imagined to be far too similar to an experience of the sense world – and therefore what is experienced when reading about this world is far too close to the nature of thought. But if we have *truly* absorbed these thoughts we are already within this world, and have only fully to realize that what we thought we had received merely as an intellectual communication has already been experienced unnoticed.' [32]

An important part of 'true' absorption through thought of this kind of subject matter is of course the acquisition of 'Michaelic' thinking: the infusing of thinking with the right kind of feeling. The reader has to achieve this independently by means of 'energetic thinking work', however, rather than having it subliminally suggested to him by the writer. Steiner's presentations continue therefore to be matter-of-fact and factual, even when he is dealing with the highest realms of existence. We can nevertheless become aware, if we engage closely and intimately with the text, that these sober presentations also arose originally from a thinking infused by reverent feelings. You can notice, for instance, that in his new style of writing about religious ideas, even when they are described as wrong-headed, Steiner no longer speaks dismissively or with brisk rejection – as happened now and again in his earlier publications. Much can be learnt likewise from the later additions and stylistic corrections he made for new editions of his earlier works. A classic example in this respect is his correction at the end of the original preface to his *Philosophy of Freedom*. In the first edition the final sentence ran: 'We must *master* the thought, *otherwise* we will be enslaved by it.' That sounds compelling and seems eminently understandable, yet it is not compatible with a thinking infused with reverence. So in 1918 Steiner corrects this, saying: 'We must be able to engage with the thought as *experience*, for *otherwise* we will be enslaved by it.' The new juxtaposition of 'experience' and 'enslavement' is at first glance not clearly comprehensible at all. Reading it, our normal way of thinking is again disorientated. Not until we make further attempts to understand it will we discover that to speak of 'experience' here is to sum up the whole significance of 'pure thinking' in the manner in which the *Philosophy of Freedom* deals with it, namely the process of acquiring consciousness of the spirit within our own formulation of thoughts. If you scrutinize Steiner's style in detail you will discover that 'Michaelic' thinking means sense-free thinking inwardly warmed and illumined by the sun of reverence.

Already in chapter 1 of this book, we rejected the idea that someone active as an initiate today has an advance plan detailing everything relating to his earthly mission, and only needs to work out his actual strategies – what he should say first and what later in accordance with humanity's state of maturity. Our account aims to show that the biography of an individual such as Rudolf Steiner follows substantially different laws. If we wish to explore this in greater detail we could say something like this: An initiate is certainly born with an extraordinary wealth of wisdom, part of which comes from previous incarnations, and part of which – depending also on what he acquired in this way – is enhanced and supplemented by a gift of grace from higher spheres. He brings with him a capacity for conscious spiritual vision and an overflowing potential for sacrifice. Like everyone else, during childhood he must gradually make his bodily sheaths into a fitting instrument for his earthly task. And like everyone else, likewise, he must try, in subsequent years, to discover the true impulses of his 'I', and bring them to realization. But this 'I' does not speak to him primarily as a kind of 'inner voice'; instead it reveals itself to him, as to everyone else, largely in the events of his destiny. The greatness of an individual such as Rudolf Steiner does not lie in some absolute certainty which he possesses from the outset so that he only has to reach within to find whatever is needed at any moment. On the contrary, he possesses the greatest ability to identify himself consciously with his destiny, to allow his higher 'I' to pour into him from and through his destiny. His destiny sets him tasks, which in truth are set him by his true 'I'.

Steiner takes hold of these tasks with utter devotion and with his whole capacity for sacrifice. As described in his autobiography, therefore, a series of outer promptings show him the need, as his first task, to develop thinking so that it can potentially receive the spirit, despite the fact that thinking had become entirely void of spirit in the modern age. To do this he had to turn contemporary thinking in an entirely new direction, so to speak preparing a new river bed for humanity's stream of thought. Understandably, this could not happen through any sort of grandiose dispensation of spiritual treasures, but only by means of the hardest and most intense spiritual work, by consciously withdrawing from all that connected him with external reality. He was thus able to point the way to a grasp of thinking as such, to an experience of 'pure thinking'.

In a similar way at a later date, when destiny – that is, his 'I' – made him a spiritual teacher, he found himself confronted with the new task of opening thinking to receive detailed spiritual facts. This involved consistent further development of the delicate seeds of moral thinking, which start to light up at the stage of sense-free thinking. To help people immersed in the outer sense world to understand the superabundant moral content of spiritual spheres, it was necessary to create the possibility of at least partly grasping conscious hold of this moral content in the soul's mirroring of thoughts infused with reverence. Once again Steiner had to inaugurate an entirely new way of forming thoughts. First of all he himself acquired this new mode, developing from it a new way of expressing himself, as we see in his spiritual scientific works. This again took years of work – not a great deal of time, in fact, if one considers that we, who strive to be his pupils, need a whole lifetime to change only a small part of our thinking in this way! Thus a second new level of thinking was made accessible to humankind.

If we try to inwardly trace how, during these years, Steiner accomplishes one new step after another with enormous energy out of his higher 'I', the idea of accusing him of being inconsistent or even of having a contradictory worldview can scarcely be maintained. What he actually did at that time was lay down a path for the whole of humanity for a new way of forming thoughts; and at the same time he gave us all an example of enormous devotion to destiny.

Yet what he accomplished around the turn of the century had its true roots in a much earlier period, a thousand years previously. In his karma lectures[33] he speaks about the discourses that took place between particular individuals in the ninth century in the supersensible world. Some of these were working to further Aristotelian impulses in a Christian way, while others sought to perpetuate Arabic monotheism in a rigidified form. From these discourses arose decisions which led to the thought life of modern times initially being informed by the latter stream; and thus a head-bound, spirit-alien thinking developed. Not until the dawn of the new age of Michael's rulership, towards the end of the nineteenth century, did it become possible for the Christian-Aristotelian stream – whose foremost representative was Steiner himself – to come into its own. The task this stream now has is to inherit the previous mode of thinking and, in Christianizing it, turn it in a spiritual direction. So Steiner's achievement around the turn of the last century was to accomplish something which he had already undertaken to support a thousand years before. Through the series of events with which his destiny presented him, his higher ego awoke in him anew the memory of his task.

Five

The Third Step:
Love

The Michael impulse expresses itself in thinking activity through the participation of feeling impulses in the forming of thoughts. This does not, of course, mean that thinking is influenced, or even worse dominated by subjective, self-centred emotions, or by feelings that arise 'of themselves' alongside thinking, or by personal sympathies or the joys of mental discovery. On the contrary, wonder, admiration and reverence for what we seek to understand, when included as an essential part of this process, are feelings that in no way dim our power of understanding, but transform it into a purer, more receptive vessel for the essential nature of reality. Thoughts informed by feeling can inevitably work back more deeply upon our inner life than shadowy 'head' thoughts; and by thus participating in the forming of thoughts, inner life will itself also be directly infused and purified by these thoughts: the feeling sphere is momentarily lifted out of its usual subjectivity and can, through patient and repeated practice, become ever more strongly influenced by this objectivity of thought. Where feelings work in an ennobling way on thinking, thinking for its part can work in a refining, ennobling way on feeling, overcoming its tendency to be self-centred.

We have already remarked that the sphere of feeling cannot be easily confined or defined in its diverse modes of soul expression. In one direction, its waves can flow beyond its dreamy domain and approach the area of clearly conscious thinking; and in the other direction it can work down into almost, or entirely, subconscious depths of will. The extent to which the interrelationship between feeling and thinking reaches down into the deep sources that shape our moral life, the impulses of love, the courage for sacrifice, and all the other germinal powers of moral action, depends on the dedicated intensity of spiritual endeavour. By this means the will can also participate in our grasp of meaning and the forming of our thought content. This kind of involvement of the will can be called the *third level of thinking's approach to the spirit.* At this level the 'whole human being' actually participates in thinking. In what way does this alter it? How does this new step take place, and how do we experience it within ourselves?

Here we enter a realm where it becomes increasingly difficult to communicate in words. We can however clarify this stage by comparing it with another area of experience. Goethe's *Theory of Colour* contains the marvellous chapter on colour's 'sensory-moral effect', in which Goethe shows that the effect of colours on those open to them arouses certain feelings governed by quite specific laws. Such feelings are by no means an expression of our subjective relationship to a particular colour but, on the contrary, express the real nature of the colour in a new and deeper way. Just as sense impressions give us an objective, *external* picture of the colour, in this way we can receive an objective *soul* picture of it. With an appropriate openness of soul, each colour triggers a different mood in us, a different answer in the form of a feeling. Thus in the feeling realm, too, we find we can engage objectively with colours. Feelings here become cognitive organs.

In this sense Goethe states that the colour yellow 'has a cheerful, lively, gently stimulating effect', and that 'it makes a thoroughly warm and comforting impression'. And he confirms this, among other things, by an experiment in which he looked at a landscape through yellow glass, especially on grey days in winter. He did similar things with the rest of the colours of the spectrum.

Let us try to carry Goethe's experiment further in a certain direction. If you put the yellow glass aside again and see the world in its natural colours, that is, when you are exposed again to quite different feelings, then the feeling experience we have just described fades again. But something else might occur. With some degree of practice you can strengthen this short-lived colour experience, get it to become ever clearer so that you can hold onto it for a short time, even if the yellow filter is no longer there. And now you just need to continue the exercise by filling yourself more and more intensively with the experience of yellow: try to hold onto the feeling consciously for a long time, and see the world entirely in this mood, so that it enters into your very words and actions. Once you have completely identified with the experience of yellow, for a short while at least the mood of yellow becomes your whole mood, raying out from within you and penetrating even your outward conduct.

And then, instead of doing this with yellow, we can do something similar with red. Initially we may find that the 'pleasant, cheerful feeling that we get with this red-yellow increases to the point of being unbearably powerful'. If we now fill ourselves entirely with this impression of red we can encounter the world as pure cholerics. The colour enters right into the way our temperament expresses itself.

In both cases, the way we feel about the colour makes itself felt right into our volition, our expressions of will, so that the latter participates in this deeper colour experience. Only then, in fact, can we speak of a 'moral' effect of colour, through being so infused with the initial, delicate colour experience that it can influence us right into the morality expressed in our actions. In this way we could imagine a whole spectrum of inner, colour-related ways of looking at things that we could awaken within us – in each case in association with the memory of a particular colour – and enact fully consciously, thus engaging with the world in ever-new transformations of soul.

But now let us turn back from perceiving colour to forming thoughts. We characterized the way the heart participates in thinking by first describing a general feeling of reverence which can resonate through our thoughts. Such warmth of feeling can change thoughts from being usurpers of knowledge to vessels humbly raised to receive knowledge deeply and gratefully. We spoke of how the contents of knowledge themselves bring a great differentiation into the feelings of reverence active in thinking. In our comparison, this process would be analogous to the engendering of different objective feelings when perceiving different colours. Just as each colour produces a specific feeling experience, in this case a different thought content gives a different nuance or shade of feeling to the vessels of reverence raised towards it. We evolve a differentiated feeling relationship to the diversity of knowledge. Every concept, every sentence, every section of a spiritual scientific article should – when worked at in a concentrated, energetic, fully conscious way – find its echo, its individual answer, in a different feeling correspondence. This mutual correspondence, again, is what makes possible a grasp of spiritual facts illumined by reality. We described this step as the second stage of the spiritualization of thinking.

We also spoke of the fact, however, that concepts themselves always contain seeds of morality. The feeling 'echo' or resonance of the second stage starts to give this moral content a more vivid reality: we can sense the actual correspondence of beings and realms of being with the depths of our own inner life. For the hidden moral seeds to unfold within us, however, with increasingly tangible clarity, we must come to the point of offering them not only the diversity of our reverential feelings but also our own moral capacities, the impulses of will corresponding to the object of knowledge. In other words, we must endeavour to meet morality with morality, and inwardly reflect it.

In practical terms this means devoting ourselves with as much intensity and focus as we can muster to a thought content that is as far as possible sense-free, to the meaning of a thought: listening in to it lovingly, feeling one with it. If, in this way, we also begin to engage our will in our thinking, an organ of perception for the otherwise concealed moral content of ideas will open in our hearts.

Every act of knowing contains an inherent, concealed moral impulse – insofar as we do not, by habit, push knowledge away into the realm of abstractions but are prepared to experience it. To give a simple, possibly somewhat primitive example, take the concept of 'gravity' and try to enter right into it in a thinking-feeling way with the described inner devotion. You will then experience the gravitational pull of matter as a kind of 'implacable clutching hold of something'. Understood in this way, the concept's content begins to have a relation to the realm of moral values. And you will know immediately that if you were to permit this form of the concept to assert its full nature in your own life and actions, it would become an unquenchable, dragon-like greed. What appears to be a dry concept in the realm of physics suddenly acquires an affinity with what we otherwise know as immorality, indeed as subjection to powers adversarial to human evolution.

Or focus on the concept 'dandelion'. You can inwardly picture the way the dandelion first of all extends its rosette of leaves in all directions, then raises its stem straight upwards, and finally turns its blossom towards the sun, becoming itself an image of the sun. If the sun is not shining the blossom closes, unwilling to allow influences other than those of the sun to affect it. But in the closed blossoms seeds form that will take the dandelion into the future. The essence of the dandelion, which can be grasped by thinking, is of a living harmony, a living unity of all these aspects. By means of intensive, devotional thinking, all these externally enumerated features can be mirrored in us as sensory-moral impulses: the striving to reach out in all directions, the longing for transparent openness to light's life forces, the longing to become an image of this life-giving light, allowing the fruit to ripen for the future in inner seclusion. We are characterizing these things symbolically here, but the important point is not to present them externally, but to awaken orienting impulses in ourselves.

When will forces work in this way on the forming of thoughts, the latter are deepened and strengthened to the point of developing moral substance. We can then experience them not only as *spiritually real*, but, with increasing clarity, as *living beings*.

THE THIRD STEP: LOVE

Let us recall once again the stages of practice that have led us to the present level. Thinking first had to confront itself. Then it had to become a reverential vessel to receive supersensible content. Finally it had to find resonance in its own depths of will. In this process, 'reflective' thinking increasingly becomes 'meditative' thinking which increasingly enters the domain characterized by Steiner in relation to meditation:

'We are now immersed in a world of thought. We must develop a *living feeling* for this silent thinking activity. We must learn to *love* what the spirit pours into us. We will soon cease to feel that this thought world is less real than the everyday things that surround us. We begin to relate to our thoughts as to things in space. And the moment approaches when we begin to feel that what reveals itself in the silent, inward thought world is much greater, much more real than things in space. We discover that *life* expresses itself in this thought world. We discover that our thoughts do not merely exist as shadow pictures, but that, through them, hidden *beings* speak to us. Out of the silence, speech becomes audible to us...'[34]

'To develop a living feeling', 'to learn to love'; do we recognize here the two steps on the path we are pursuing as we develop our thinking? What is said here about meditation can – even if in a somewhat humbler way – become our own experience on the path presented here for cultivating esoteric thoughts. We have seen how, even on the first step of this path, we can discover the *reality* of the thought world. And by confronting our own thinking as an observer we also acquire the capacity – almost unnoticeably to start with, and ever more consciously later on – 'to relate to our thoughts as to things in space'. We have also seen how, at the second level, by including feeling, we can acquire a living versatility and mobility in the content of thought; this is when we start to discover *life* in the thought world. And finally we saw that at the third level we can experience the reality of thoughts increasingly as *living substance*. Here we come ever closer to the experience of hearing, in the meaning of facts grasped by thinking, the silent *speech of hidden beings*. 'Meditative thinking' can convey all these experiences. How these experiences differ from those of meditation as such will be described in the chapter on the 'Fourth Step'.

Let us return once more to our comparison with the 'sensory-moral' effect of colour. The third level of thinking's spiritualization would correspond to complete inner immersion in a colour mood, so that we experience it as our own moral strength. The participation of will forces that are otherwise slumbering and hidden is similar in both cases. In both instances an increase in the intensity of the original feeling experience is involved. There is, however, a highly characteristic difference.

Referring to Goethe's theory of colour, we considered the possibility of connecting so intensely with the feeling impression of a colour that for a while the soul is entirely filled by it, and it comes to dominate our whole mood and outlook on life. Now one could imagine – theoretically at least – that something similar could occur with the intuitions in our life of thinking: in other words, we could grasp hold of the spiritual gesture we experience in a particular thought intuition so intensely that it merges with our own character, becoming part of it. For example, if we were to immerse our whole inner being in the concept of 'gravity' we might then be filled by an infinite, egotistic greed. That might be conceivable, but in actuality this does not happen because the whole course of our prior training in thought protects us

THE THIRD STEP: LOVE

against it. By working on our thinking we develop impulses, as a matter of course, which entirely exclude selfish emotions during our observation of thinking. Already at the first stage of inner work on thinking, we develop forces of active and pure devotion to our thought content – forces which otherwise, in the ordinary mode of thinking, do not appear at all. These devotional forces increase at the second level, and become fully manifest at the third level as pure forces of love. We do indeed radiate love as we engage in thinking contemplation. Immoral, selfish will impulses would never enable us to uncover the deeper secrets of the thought world. The ability to perceive our thoughts' moral gestures is born only when we combine these thoughts with the strongest moral forces we can muster.

Admittedly, in the process of perceiving these gestures, we become temporally 'one' with them, but this does not mean we are ever possessed by them, even momentarily; we remain *free* while we experience them. We open ourselves to the moral substance of our thoughts, certainly, but then we always decide in freedom how we should relate to them. Whether we decide to put into action an insight acquired in this way, or whether we concentrate on uniting the moral concept of a thought, such as the dandelion striving towards the light, with the depths of our soul so that it becomes a soul impulse, or whether we only take quiet note of the moral aspect we have grasped from it: on each occasion this is up to the free decision of the thinking individual.

The view we have of the world undergoes a radical change at this stage. At the level of ordinary thinking the outer world appears to us as morally indifferent, ruled solely by natural laws unconcerned with morality, while moral laws are considered to be artificial, human additions, of solely personal value. At the third level of thought's deepening, when love streams into our efforts to understand the world, we notice ever more clearly that the web of thoughts, without which the world is not real to us of course, is absolutely full of morality, so that even the visible world now contains morality wherever we look. The sense world increasingly becomes a moral world. Wherever we look, the world stimulates us morally, which means that we feel as though the world were talking to us, and sense that something is expected of us. We can no longer live our lives as if we are unnoticed strangers, cut off from the world, as though indifferent to it, unconnected with it – and therefore entitled not to be interested in it either. In fact we might now even say that the world bombards us continually, everywhere challenging us with the question: what are you, as the person you now are, going to do? Alongside this omnipresent question, moral inspirations also flow into us, which we can take up into our moral imagination and transform into action.

So now – and probably not before – we can fully experience what is described and psychologically demonstrated in the *Philosophy of Freedom*: the birth of a free deed out of pure thinking, the transformation of purest knowledge into purest morality. Love for the objective reality of the world, which thinking reveals to us, can give rise to free and truly moral action.

In engaging repeatedly with the moral content of thoughts, human beings are gradually developing their aptitude for independent morality. The world manifests its moral content to us everywhere, and human beings increasingly become a pure mirror, a microcosm of this morality, the human expression, in a new, deep sense, of the world's manifestation.

This is also what Michael expects of human beings:

'By feeling themselves to be free beings in Michael's presence, human beings are on the way to supporting their intellectual forces with the whole of their being; although we think with our heads, our hearts feel the light and shade of our thinking; and our will emanates our being where thoughts stream through us in the form of intentions. In becoming an expression of the world we increasingly become a real human being. We find ourselves not by *looking for* ourselves, but by connecting ourselves lovingly with the world.

'Those loyal to Michael are cultivating a loving relationship to the outer world, and by doing so they find the relation to their soul's inner world, which brings them to the Christ.'[35]

It is important to note that the love spoken of here unfolds when people's 'thoughts stream through them in the form of intentions' and when this makes them 'an expression of the world'. This is the completely new plane of Christianity, only accessible since the beginning of the Michael Age – Michaelic Christianity, the new possibility of being a son of God by acting out of the divine ground of the soul.

By penetrating the external veils that hide the spirit, and the world of dead, morally inert natural laws, we can indeed experience the presence of a world of ideas interwoven with morality. This world of ideas is no longer cut off from the sense world, is not beyond the sense world but embodies the true reality of this sense world. The sense world in which we have our ordinary experience of the world is merely the last, dead reflection of this reality. As we go deeper we become aware that we have taken the first steps from a dead world robbed of spirit into a world of resurrection in spirit. In this world there is no longer a 'this world' and a 'beyond', only a single world of *all-encompassing spiritual and moral reality* extending from the unfathomable, fiery depths of God's love – in the presence of which human thoughts must become powerless – to the insubstantial, surface world which our ordinary consciousness knows as the sense world. By taking this step we discover that the sense world is not only filled with spirit in the sense of a morally indifferent framework of concepts, but that it is imbued with substantial morality. Morality is experienced objectively as the content of the world.

Reaching this insight, we acquire access at a wholly new level to the fundamental view underpinning the *Philosophy of Freedom* and Steiner's earlier works as epistemological theory: There are not two worlds, a material and a spiritual one, but one homogenous unity, the basic spiritual content of which we open up through our thinking. Yet this homogenous world actually also contains the whole moral cosmos. Our ordinary thinking has no access to it, and therefore moral impulses are to begin with transposed solely into our inner being. At the third stage of thinking, however, it is not only truth that is discovered to be the objective content of the world, but morality also. Now, for the first time, the world becomes a true unity for us.

As soon as we give serious attention to this conviction of the unity of existence then we find that all apparent contradictions between Steiner's pre-anthroposophical and anthroposophical presentations are conclusively resolved, right into his specific formulations. In both instances he emphasizes the unity and the homogeneity of the world. When we think, admittedly, we are still living within the sense world, yet 'the spiritual nature of things is reflected in our thought world; and as thinking beings of spirit we are citizens of the country of spirit beings and comrades of everything that lives in this realm.'[36] We can add that we are comrades, too, of universal morality, of the love of God that permeates all things with warmth.

Steiner endeavoured, as we know, to make accessible to thinking ever new strata of this reality of moral, spiritual existence, but always in the sense of a single, unified world.

When, as we live our way into spiritual knowledge, the regions of spiritual, moral reality appear to begin with to be hidden 'behind' the sense world, this is always only an understandable initial feeling, which precedes our really getting to know these regions. If spiritual perception accesses them, their manifold connection with the sense world becomes apparent; this truth, however, is also accessible to will-sustained thinking:

'It is like a piece of ice floating on water – the ice consists of the same substance as the surrounding water but emerges from it because of certain qualities it possesses. In the same way, sense perceptible things are of the same substance as the soul and spirit worlds surrounding them, but they stand out because of certain characteristics that make them perceptible to our senses. To put it somewhat figuratively, they are condensed spirit and soul formations, and the condensation makes it possible for our senses to acquire knowledge about them. Ice is just one of the manifestations of water, and sense-perceptible things are just one form in which soul and spirit beings exist. Having grasped this, we can also understand that the spirit world can change into the soul world, and the soul world into the sensory world, just as water can turn to ice... Only because sense perceptible things are nothing other than condensed spirit beings can we human beings – who can raise ourselves in thought to the level of spirit beings – think about and understand them.'[37]

From childhood on, Steiner was able to experience the spiritual world alongside the sense world – although their connection was not to begin with clear to him: he also had to work hard to reach a view of their unity. It was for this very reason that he fought so vehemently against all forms of dualism, and every theory that spoke of a realm of existence in 'the beyond' that was inaccessible to human knowledge.

In 1897, for instance, he wrote: 'Christianity finds in God the source of everything of a spiritual nature – and thus also concepts and ideas. It needs to believe in something that is not of this world. But sound human thinking keeps hold of this world. It is not concerned with any other.'[38]

It is tempting to place the main emphasis in such a statement on the word 'God'. For Steiner, however, it fell on the phrase 'something that is not of this world'. We do not understand God if we transpose Him to an inaccessible realm; God's love is also to be found in every region of the sense world.

In Steiner's view, this statement can be juxtaposed with a later one without any contradiction. In 1918 Steiner spoke of our relationship with the Father God, that is, the godhead that primarily works and reveals itself in the physical realm. He said:

'Spiritual science shows us that human beings who deny the Father God, thus entirely denying the existence of a divine presence in the world – such as the God recognized in the religion of the Israelites – are suffering from a genuine physical defect, a physical illness in their physical body; the body lacks something. To be an atheist means, for a spiritual scientist, being ill in some form.'[39]

In both instances Steiner was trying to say the same thing: that a healthy way of regarding the world is to feel it as a spiritual-physical unity – though today most people only gradually work their way through to this feeling of unified matter and spirit. As long as we remain caught up in intellectual thinking, we have no tangible means of accessing this unity and are thus ill, in Steiner's sense. Even where we accept this at the level of philosophically 'pure' thinking, this will scarcely be sufficient to give us a natural feeling for it. Not until we reach the stage of seeing the world morally can we really inhabit this sense of unity, so that the sense world itself starts to radiate morality, in other words becomes spiritually radiant. Then at last the split between matter and spirit is resolved for us, in the experience we have described as the world's spiritual resurrection from its previous, death-allied state of insubstantiality or 'beinglessness'. In all of Rudolf Steiner's work we can hear these joyous tones of resurrection. In this sense anthroposophy is the great call to humanity to enter into the realm of resurrection, the world that is illumined and pervaded by the light of the spirit.

Knowledge steeped in love as the key that opens the gate to this realm was something Steiner expressed with special clarity in 1923:

'Unless you combine knowledge with love you cannot acquire the kind of knowledge given by anthroposophy, for otherwise such knowledge remains the same as anything else... you cannot acquire such knowledge if it is not accompanied by the feeling, the state of soul, that lives in love. If you fill your knowledge with the experience of love, then this knowledge will approach the Mystery of Golgotha. Then we not only have an – in itself – entirely justified, naïve feeling for Christ – and I do mean that it is entirely justified – but also the sort of knowledge that extends across the whole cosmos, and which can become profound enough to comprehend the Mystery of Golgotha. In other words: Life in the Holy Ghost leads to life in, or in the presence of Christ, the Son of God.'[40]

I'd like to repeatedly stress that the path leading from ordinary intellectual thinking to the resurrection realm of love-filled, Christianized thinking is lengthy and demanding. It is demanding primarily because our waking consciousness is continually pervaded by the kind of head-only knowledge instilled into us. We perceive objects – chairs, cupboards, windows, houses, trees – but we only perceive them as objects because our thinking has grown used to selecting the perceptions we seek from the general confusion of percepts, and collating or summarizing them as objects. Nor do we expect thinking to do anything other than to produce, as though by magic, an object that we can clearly distinguish from ourselves as belonging to an outer world. At every moment of our waking day, therefore, our waking consciousness is a product of our intellect. By means of this constant and mostly unnoticed thinking activity our ego secures for itself an inner distance from things, the capacity to orientate itself in its surroundings; and, besides that, an alert relationship with its environment. The periods when we – while studying spiritual-scientific books, for instance – deliberately take our thinking in hand, and equip it with impulses drawn from deeper regions of soul, form comparatively rare and festive moments in the course of the day: just isolated oases in the midst of a parched desert; and they ask us to consciously engage our will. These moments, however, are precisely when we can enter into a Christian experience of the world in a new way. And even if such festive moments of thinking are initially isolated ones, what we gain from them can, in the course of time, filter through into other moments of the day, enabling our heart to participate more strongly in our thinking.

In his lecture on 'The Etherisation of the Blood' Rudolf Steiner describes how, in our ordinary, intellectually governed waking consciousness, etheric rays, rays of light, are constantly passing from our heart to our head. In the night, while we are asleep, and when our daytime experiences are, with the help of the spiritual world, being transformed into moral impulses, other streams of light, moving in the other direction, ray in from without, from the macrocosm, through the head region towards the heart. Under normal circumstances we cannot consciously influence this macrocosmic stream – which involves the transformation of knowledge into moral impulses – unless, as Steiner says, we gradually 'bring the fire of enthusiasm into the stream that flows from the heart to the head, so that an understanding of anthroposophy awakens'. To put it differently, the 'I' lives in the blood, and must draw on the etheric stream passing from heart to head in order to think – that is, on both the etheric forces and the physical brain. But the 'I' can also introduce morally-inspired forces into waking consciousness, if, as it struggles to understand anthroposophy, it fires thinking with forces of feeling and will. What really occurs here? Rudolf Steiner says this about it:

'During the day people are awake in their intellect whereas during sleep they are awake in their will. Being asleep in their intellect they are not conscious of what they undertake with their will... What is in us can carry us forward a little intellectually, but to take a step forward in moral improvement we need help from the gods. This is why we fall asleep, so that we can be submerged in the divine will, where we are not present with our powerless intellect, and where divine forces transform into will forces what we take in as moral principles, thus inoculating with our will what we otherwise can receive only in our thoughts...

'When one observes people today clairvoyantly in their waking state, one sees certain rays of light continually moving from heart to head... Like rays of light these flow up from the heart to the head and stream around the pineal gland. These streams arise through the fact that human blood, which is a physical substance, is constantly dissolving into etheric substance, so that in the region of the heart the blood constantly changes into etheric substance streaming up into the head... But it is different when people are asleep. It is like this: if the brain is here and the heart region there, the occult observer sees a constant stream coming in from without, and from behind, into the heart...

'What one sees, in fact, are to a great degree moral qualities, in the specific colouring they assume when they stream into sleeping human beings ...

'Just as our blood streams as ether upwards from the heart, in the earth's ether since the Mystery of Golgotha lives the etherised blood of Christ Jesus. The etheric body of the earth is imbued with what became of the blood that flowed on Golgotha... This means that since the Mystery of Golgotha it is continually possible for the effect of Christ's etheric blood to mingle with these streams moving from below upwards... The human blood stream and the blood stream of Christ Jesus meet one another. But a connection between these two streams will come about only when human beings bring a right understanding to what the Christ impulse contains.'

Steiner tells us that this understanding is acquired differently today from the way it once was.

'It is important for our time that people come to realize that they need to absorb knowledge of a spiritual-scientific nature so that they gradually introduce into the stream passing from the heart to the brain sufficient fire and enthusiasm to enable them to understand anthroposophy.'

Then Steiner speaks about the new proximity of Christ, who is becoming active in etheric form among humankind. And he goes on to say: 'What will be brought about by progress in humankind's development is that the two poles I mentioned before, the intellectual and the moral, will increasingly become one, and merge.'[41]

This combining of the moral element and the sphere of knowledge is then described as the effect of Christ's presence in the etheric. Christ connects the macrocosmic moral stream with the intellectual etheric stream in human beings when this stream is filled with the fire of the spirit. In other words, at the third level of thinking we prepare our own etheric stream of thought to unite with the Christ stream. Knowledge and virtue no longer form two separate areas of soul activity, but flow together as one. Connecting the two has already been presented and philosophically established in the *Philosophy of Freedom*. This possibility, however, can continually assume ever more tangible forms. In our description of the second and third level of thinking's spiritualization we endeavoured to show that knowledge and morality can come ever closer to one another as one way to attain real spiritual community and collaboration with the etheric Christ now present within humankind.

Thus, by pursuing the path whose beginning and direction is mapped out for us in the *Philosophy of Freedom*, and invoking ever deeper soul forces, we are led firstly into the sphere of Michael – where cosmic intelligence is transformed by love and streams back towards Michael – and secondly into the sphere of Christ which dawns as living, golden ground and radiance behind the sphere of Michael: that is, as the resurrection kingdom reconciling the realms of spirit and matter, of knowledge and morality.

This experience begins with the impregnation of thinking with will and moral impulses; that is, with the third stage of the path we are describing here. But to avoid following merely abstract schemas, we should also say that the transition from the second to the third level is no longer as incisive as that from the first to the second level, but flows on almost imperceptibly from it. We spoke of how indistinct the boundary is between feeling life and will forces urging us to engage in action. The stronger a feeling is, the greater its innate tendency to prompt us to take particular actions, or at least adopt a particular stance. A strong feeling experience at the same time influences the will. This is true not only of subjective, personal feelings however, but also of the kind of feeling acquired on the path of self-development in thinking – arising therefore from conscious dedication to an objective thought reality.

If we set out, for example, to form the concept of an angel that does not remain in the shadowy realm of abstraction, we must – aware that this concerns a being superior to us – include a feeling of reverence as we form the concept. But actively attempting to understand a being ranked higher than ourselves will awaken in us will forces that are related to reverence. If we continue with our efforts, trying to make our image of the angel ever clearer and more real, we can only do so by invoking the aid of our moral potential. We could, for instance, dwell on the idea that angels do not try to pursue their own personal intentions but only those of beings higher than them, who work through them. This being so, they do everything in their power to enable us human beings to realize in our own lives the divinely willed intentions of our eternal, higher 'I'. We can only make this thought real by accompanying it with the impetus to become, at the same time, transparent for these divinely-willed intentions and seek to allow them to flow into our life on earth: in other words, to serve divine will in the same way in which angels do.

Working at spiritual scientific knowledge in this way, the very facts themselves will lead us not only to involve our feeling but also our will forces. If it is not to remain an empty phrase to say that we put our 'whole hearts' into anthroposophy, we will have to work to transform the way we form our thoughts.

Gradually, as our knowledge of anthroposophy grows, we will become aware that the concept 'human being' is something we have to work our way through to once more; that at the very core of anthroposophy stands the mysterious secret of the human being, of his true nature, origin and goals. The cosmic profundity and full sacredness of this apparently so hackneyed and misused concept has to be rediscovered and understood anew, step by step, as something grounded in eternity. All the pictures, images and visions given us by anthroposophy ought to culminate finally in a new, emergent image of the human that we can approach anew with reverence for and love of the spirit. The Goetheanum statue of 'The Representative of Humanity' likewise urges us to develop a spiritualized view of the human being; it appeals to us to become aware that the higher self of every human being bears not only a memory of our divine origin, not only the vision of a future willed for us by the gods, but also the living presence of the risen one in battle with adversarial powers. The way we view the human being, our fellow human beings and humankind awaits a resurrection of the kind of knowledge that will be ever more Christian. In 1923, shortly after the first Goetheanum burned down, Rudolf Steiner expressed this in very moving words:

'Ideas are not formed in anthroposophy the way they have previously been formed in the realm of knowledge for the past three, four or five centuries; words are not chosen as they are chosen nowadays in other fields. Where anthroposophy is concerned, ideas are vessels fashioned by love, bringing down to us in a spiritual way, from spiritual worlds, the essential nature of the human being. Encompassed by lovingly formed thoughts, the light of true humanity will shine forth from anthroposophy. And knowledge is merely the way in which, through human beings, the capacity will arise for the true spirit to descend from the breadths of the cosmos and gather in human hearts, so that, emanating from human hearts, this spirit can illumine human thoughts. And because anthroposophy can really only be grasped through love, it creates love when human beings grasp its true nature... And in the realm of anthroposophy words are not coined as they are otherwise coined nowadays, but are really receiving vessels. Every word in anthroposophy is, if spoken rightly, really a plea, a reverent plea for the spirit to descend to human beings.' [42]

Six

Interlude:
'Living Thinking'

Steiner frequently draws our attention to the importance of 'living concepts', a living thinking, as distinct from the rigid and dead abstract thinking that is widespread. We also repeatedly find references to 'living thinking' in anthroposophical literature since Steiner's time. When we first read these words we usually think we understand them. But do we really?

What do we conceive 'living thinking' to be? The sort of thing that, for instance, combines logic with flights of fancy? Or thinking accompanied by brightly-coloured mental images? Or the kind of thinking that does not strictly adhere to a logical train but is willing to depart from it at any moment? Or perhaps a thinking sufficiently mobile to engage with any field of knowledge, seeking to relate fruitfully to the desired conclusions? Or thinking accompanied by violent emotions? Or does one perhaps credit every effort to engage with anthroposophical ideas as being automatically 'living'?

None of these ways of thinking would be particularly useful for working with anthroposophy. And on closer examination, they really do not have anything in common with real 'living' thinking either.

When Steiner gave introductory lectures to the future teachers of the first Steiner Waldorf School in 1919, he spoke in somewhat more detail about what he meant by the expression 'living concepts'. This took place as part of a discussion on logic – on concepts, judgements and conclusions. He said:

'If, at the age of nine or ten, you inculcate into children concepts that are intended to be still in them in the same form when they are thirty or forty, you are inculcating dead concepts, which do not go on living with them as they grow and develop. You have to teach children the kinds of concept that transform through their lives. Teachers must take care to convey to children the sort of concept that does not remain as it was when first given them, but can transform in later life. If you do that, then you are giving children living concepts. You are filling them with dead concepts whenever you present them with definitions. If you say: A lion is… and so on, and let them learn that by heart, you are giving them dead concepts; and you can be assured that when they are thirty these concepts will still be there in them in exactly the same form in which they learnt them … So what must you do? We should not spend lessons defining things, but trying to *characterize* instead. We can characterize by trying to present things from as many points of view as possible.

'If we simply teach children in natural history lessons what we find about animals in today's natural history books, we are only defining them. We have to try, in every part of the lesson, to describe animals from different aspects; for instance, how people gradually came to know about these animals, to make use of their capacities, and so on. These relationships will be so multi-faceted that a characterization will arise instead of a mere definition. Teaching properly sets out not to define but to characterize.'[43]

Firstly, what we can gather here is that the living nature of concepts involves their capacity to continue to develop as young people grow and mature. Secondly, that we can arrive at these living concepts by trying to observe things from different points of view. What does this desire to understand things from different aspects have to do with the 'living nature' of concepts?

Let us remind ourselves that our thoughts are shadow images of the spiritual archetypes that reside in 'spirit land', and (recalling the quotation on page 33) that these archetypal images reveal themselves in forms that are continually changing, that they are more or less related to other archetypal images, and continually connecting with them, thus giving rise to one or another being in the soul world or physical world. This interconnecting lattice of archetypal images in spirit land can be recognized by the way it expresses itself in the innumerable mutual connections between concepts as we know them. How many concepts are connected, for example, with a rose! To start with: root, stem, thorn, leaf, bud, blossom and fruit. Then the concept of diverse colours and forms, the concept of hardness and softness, and that of growth and decay; and also cultivating and watering. Then the concepts of: earth, water, air, light, warmth, wind, rain, shade and sunshine; and: human being, butterfly, bee, greenfly; and also: scent, oil, dewdrops, beauty and love. We could continue by examining concepts of either related or less related plants; and, to be consistent, we would eventually discover connections of all kinds, positive or negative, with every other imaginable concept. The more such relationships we can encompass in our thinking, the more we can assume that our thinking about the rose will reflect the vivid and fluctuating life of archetypal images; that it not only identifies isolated shadow images of the world of archetypes but can mirror this world with ever more faithfulness, and even become a bearer of and participant in its life.

We can, of course, gather thoughts together from as many angles as we like, from any number of facts, without having the slightest trace of life in our thinking. We can know countless details about something without its concept becoming any less rigid – because our knowledge of these things may also be dead, desiccated and inflexible. How do we succeed in recreating in our thinking, to a small extent at least, the life that exists in the wealth of colour and form of spirit land?

Here, of course, we must distinguish between children and adults. It is easier for children in this respect, because they usually do not yet have the tendency to absorb concepts abstractly – unless this tendency has already been inculcated into them by an abstract education – because they still live predominantly in feelings and creative imagination. If concepts are living and mobile in a teacher's consciousness, they will also be absorbed by children in this way, and will continue to resonate in the flux of children's feeling and imagination. So it depends entirely on the teacher whether children can think in living concepts or not.

In today's civilization it is taken for granted that adults are so steeped in the capacity for abstraction that they can scarcely acquire concepts in any other than abstract form. And even if they acquaint themselves with various aspects of things, or if, in order to avoid concepts that are too sharply defined, they accept imprecise or not fully understood concepts, these remain in their awareness in a form that is schematic, dry and lifeless. Isolated items of knowledge, which ought to supplement one another, do not cohere into a meaningful and organic whole, but remain in people's consciousness in meaningless juxtapositions.

The only remedy is to depart from traditional currents

of thought and set about transforming one's thinking. We already know the redeeming magic word – 'reverence' – which releases thoughts from their fatal enchantment. Infusing our thinking with impulses of feeling removes the dividing lines between concepts or even whole thought sequences, so that concepts open up to one another and form a whole host of interconnections, becoming more fluid and mobile in the process. And if things are then observed from various perspectives, concepts can combine in ever new ways, and a thought life filled with feeling can mirror the surging and creative life of the archetypal images in 'spirit land'. Thus we can fulfil what Steiner urged for the second stage of deepening thinking, as quoted above.

The expression 'living thinking', however, is not necessarily restricted to that single meaning, as given in Steiner's quotation, even in Steiner's own view. We can also find ways of enlivening our thoughts at other stages of thinking's development. The first of these offers itself already at the first level; that is, at the stage of pure, sense-free thinking. Let us call to mind once again the main conclusion Steiner came to in his epistemological works. There he showed how, with careful observation of thinking activity, we can discover that the 'essence of things' becomes manifest in thought; and therefore the world becomes comprehensible to us when we add a concept to a percept. So let us concentrate on looking more exactly at this key thought – for we know, of course, that not every thought results in actual understanding. There are innumerable thoughts that pass reality by – miss the mark – or do not quite connect with it. To really understand something we need to supplement the perception we are concerned with by bringing the right, corresponding intuition to bear on it. This is often difficult, and does not inevitably succeed in each instance, and certainly not immediately. It took centuries for the fundamental laws of inorganic nature to be discovered, explained and elaborated in every detail. It took the thought activity of many generations of research scientists for us to be able to understand the physical processes occurring in the sense world, and on the basis of this understanding to exploit them specifically for human purposes.

But we have not yet by any means accomplished something similar in relation to the laws of life. And suddenly we come up here against the inexorable need for 'living concepts,' because other concepts just do not provide us with an adequate means of understanding life. These can, at most, enable us to map the dead externals of life but not life itself. This is why, fundamentally, where biology and medicine are concerned, we remain in ignorance before the riddle of living processes. We certainly try to make life subject to our control – in the breeding of new plants and animals for instance, in the speeding up or slowing down of the moment of birth, in discussions regarding brain death and euthanasia, and in the somewhat sinister realm of genetic engineering. But all this remains a dogged, blind involvement in processes we have no real insight into, messing about in the manner of the sorcerer's apprentice. We go on stubbornly and repeatedly trying in vain to understand life in terms of physical compounds and chemical reactions, invariably missing the 'manifest secret' of life (Goethe), which, however, twentieth century biologists highlighted on several occasions, and which Goethe, a long time before them, pioneered in his theory of metamorphosis and made accessible to thinking.

What is the essential quality of life? Above all its relationship with time and temporal processes. The plant I see before me is not the whole, and therefore not the real plant. It appears as a whole only when I consider the whole cycle of its development, the whole current of its transformations from seed through sprout, shoot, blossom and fruit, and back again to the seed. It is not a spatial whole but a temporal whole, an organism in time. But it is not only that. To be able to understand the changing form of plants we have to consider that their development is continually determined by influences from the soil, moisture, air, warmth and light, and also the heavens. The plant can realize its form only in constant dialogue with its environment. If these influences alter, then the plant form will also alter.

This brings us to the starting point for Goethe's plant observations: the basis on which he developed his idea of the 'archetypal plant' as an embodiment of general lawfulness that could be traced in all plants. Whilst this archetypal lawfulness always remains the same, the manifold varieties can be attributed to environmental effects of varying duration. Every actual plant form can be derived from the form of Goethe's archetypal plant, and its individual manifestation as a temporal phenomenon can be understood on this basis. This kind of general picture of an organism – the archetypal plant in the case of plants – is what Goethe called the 'type'. The type always includes innumerable possibilities of individually divergent manifestations; as an externally invisible, archetypal law it can assume the most diverse visible shapes.

Now the type is not sensory in nature, but ideal, an idea. If one wants to apply it to understand the world of organisms one has to treat it differently from the sorts of concept which relate to the lifeless world. It must become a 'living concept'. In what sense? We shall start by seeing what Steiner has to say:[44]

'The type plays the same role in the organic world as a law of nature does in the inorganic world. Just as the latter gives us the chance to see everything that happens as part of one great totality, the type puts us in the position of seeing each individual organism as a specific form of the archetype.'

What Haeckel or other naturalists regard as the archetypal form is already a special form of it, is just the simplest example of the type. The fact that, chronologically, it first appears in its simplest form does not mean that subsequent forms are the result of the previously occurring one. *All* forms are *the result of the type*: the first as well as the last are manifestations of it. A true study of organic nature must base itself on this type, rather than simply trying to derive specific animal and plant types from each other. Like a connecting thread the type runs through all the developmental stages of the organic world. We have to hold fast to it and then go along *with it,* through this tremendous realm of divergent forms. Then we shall understand it. Otherwise, as happens with all the rest of the experienced world, it will collapse in a disconnected host of details.

'A natural law expresses the connection between separate facts in the sense world; it continues to apply, however, despite the manifold separate phenomena. In the case of the type we have to trace how each particular example of it that we meet *develops out of* the archetypal form. We should not ask how the type governs each separate form, but just *develop the latter from it.* The law governs each phenomenon as something standing above it; the type flows into each living entity, identifying with it.'

Just as we attribute an inorganic phenomenon to a law, in the case of the type we *develop* a particular form out of the archetype.

How does this help us answer our question? Do Steiner's observations also contain a secret about creating living concepts? We have pointed to the fact that when we want to grasp the essential thing about a living organism we have to include a picture of its development, have to become conscious of the stages it passes through as it continually changes. So the first step towards forming the living concept of a plant is bound to be this: to practise the art of picturing, under the name of a plant, not only something like a momentary view of it in full bloom, but its whole cycle of growth, its maturing and dying. We shall find the essential nature of the rose not in the rose that we cut and put in a vase, but as a phenomenon seen in temporal sequences, through the seasons. When we look at a meadow in bloom we should connect with it the thought that all these plants are proceeding from the past towards the future; what I see at this moment is, as such, maya. And now, to pass from this *knowledge* of the manifestation of plant nature through time to *understanding* it, we must – in keeping with Steiner's explanations – get help from the type, the archetypal plant. To come to the crucial step: we are now faced with the task of *developing* the – temporal! – form of the particular plant, for instance the rose, out of the – temporal! – form of the archetypal plant; that is, to see the actual way the general lawfulness of the development of plant growth enters into this plant's particular shape; or in other words, to allow our knowledge of the general workings of etheric formative forces in plants to pass over into a grasp of the workings of etheric formative forces in the particular rose. Faced with this task, we have to occupy ourselves with certain questions, such as: How does the rose express the general principle of expansion and contraction in its leaf growth? By asking questions such as this we will also focus on environmental influences from the earth and the cosmos, without the consideration of which we would be left with a concept of the rose that would still be vague and poor in content.[45]

The crucial thing, then, is to derive the actual form of the rose from the type. This is not a logical operation. It cannot be done by means of logical conclusions. We have to apply a creatively artistic element in an evaluative process based on comparing and observing – that is, the sort of thing that as yet does not figure at all in traditional scientific thinking. The kind of capacity which a sculptor uses to create forms from clay, moulding and shaping them, must come to life in our thinking, so that we derive individually real forms from something that is general to all of them. It is clear that the concepts we are working with here have to remain plastic, open and mobile: they must be 'living' concepts; after all, the forms of living structures cannot be understood other than by means of concepts that can transform into one another. When Goethe's concept of type is introduced into nature study, scientific activities acquire features that are artistically creative. And when this happens we anticipate the 'level of reverence' of spiritual scientific thinking, at which point, through the involvement of feeling, concepts lose their rigid delimitations and can thus open to something greater. This in turn allows us – as we indicated on page 38 – to grasp the world as a work of art, as something filled with beauty.

This artistic element in thinking, which we develop in studying the plant world, appears to be a more actively creative kind, whereas sensing beauty in the world through the capacity to admire it, is more like reverent receiving. We can characterize the two ways of thinking by comparing thinking activity relating to the archetypal plant to 'form drawing' in a Steiner Waldorf School, whereas acquiring knowledge through reverential thinking is more akin to the colour experience in painting.

By letting temporal and developmental notions flow into the way we form concepts, the foundation is laid for an important deepening of our relationship as human beings with all life – plants, animals and also the human world. In every realm of life our rigidified concepts have been waiting for centuries now to revive from their frozen enchantment. To this end, we can now elaborate a theme in more tangible detail, as we touched on at the end of the previous chapter: the new capacity for insight into the mystery of the human being.

Let us start by asking what the effect on our self-knowledge will be of acquiring the kind of thinking that includes an awareness of time? Usually everyone forms for themselves a certain mental picture of their personality according to the way they are at present. When they say 'I' to themselves they normally mean the present content of their experience of themselves: the immediate state of their capacities, views, intentions, and hopes, their human relationships and their general feeling about life. In reality, however, what people are like at any moment of their lives does not give an exhaustive picture of their essential being. In the same way as the roots of a tree are an inseparable part of the tree, our past is an inseparable part of us. The way we thought, felt and lived ten, twenty or thirty years ago is still part of us. Likewise part of us is all the future potential in us that is not nurtured and developed, all initial efforts left unfinished. Without their past, people would not be what they are now. But beyond this, people do not just live in themselves, of course, in an isolated void. We are also worked upon 'from without' by strokes of destiny, and especially through experiences shared with others. Without such influences people would be inwardly different from what they actually are. And, looking back into the past in search of these influences, we find, as we penetrate further back into childhood, ever more of these decisive influences: school friends, teachers, other adults, family members and parents. What would we have been without them? In addition to these figures in our life, there are also all sorts of richly influential events of destiny and elements of our surroundings – at home, in our town or village, the mountains or the sea, and so on. When we think of our childhood surroundings, we have to remind ourselves once again that all this contributed to our developing personality; without the people, the places and landscapes, and without all that happened to me, I would not be the person I am; everything that once surrounded me is embedded in me, belongs to my 'I'. And I discover that my own being is deeply rooted in the world and in humanity as a whole. An untold number of mutually interacting influences came together in me, to form my developing personality. My whole previous development, some of which I am not even aware of, makes me what I am. My own 'I' comes shining towards me out of other human faces, out of my surroundings, from nature, and from the gifts and strokes of destiny. My momentary thoughts, attitudes and moods of soul are in truth only a momentary detail of an ongoing process determined by the past and at the same time disappearing into the future. Thus self-observation, overcoming our confinement in the present, acknowledges our past and puts faith in something new that we can still hardly picture, that will, depending on our destiny, help shape our future. In this way an image of ourselves arises in which we can no longer feel enclosed in ourselves, but know we owe our nature to other people and the whole evolutionary context of the world; and that we grow towards the future by continually receiving our own being from our surroundings.

Our consideration of developmental unfolding also affects the way we look at other people. The good or bad qualities that appear in them at present, and their present words and actions, lose part of their significance, their compelling power. Other questions take precedence, for instance: how did this person become as he is? Who or what contributed to make this come about? The characteristics we see are only a momentary glimpse into a process of growth that is developing from the past into the future, and is likewise not yet finished. Where does this process of development appear to be heading? In what way may we ourselves have affected it? What can we contribute to it in the future? However hardened and inflexible people appear to be at a given moment in their lives, we always have the opportunity to endeavour to use our thinking to grasp their essential being, their higher reality, as something still developing. Do such thoughts mean nothing; are they 'just thoughts'? Might they not also emanate helpful, therapeutic or redemptive forces? *A Christmas Carol* by Dickens presents us with an unbelievably desiccated old skinflint who, by re-experiencing his long forgotten past, learns to rediscover the former philanthropic thread of his life. In our thoughts, at least, we can repeatedly glimpse other people's potential, and in the way we relate to these people we can look for new points of emphasis in their past and future.

So far we have only been trying to include the element of time, the process of development, in our thoughts about a human being, in the way one can do this with plants by picturing their whole cycle of growth. But we also intimated that a deeper understanding of plant life can only be achieved by seeking to connect the development of a particular plant with the general archetypal image of plant growth – with the type. We can do something similar when observing human life, too. A difference here, though, is that human beings are not the realization of an archetypal evolutionary picture but individual beings in their own right, individual egos that do not derive from anything else; they are beings able to determine their own life's goals purely through their own inner dictates. And this is not altered in the least by the fact that, as we saw, human beings receive their 'I' as a gift from their surroundings as they grow and develop. In fact, we can take this mysterious connection between human beings and the world as an exhortation not to try to grasp the secrets of the 'I' with ordinary thinking but instead with the kind of thinking purified by reverence and love. If we remain aware that the essential nature of the 'I' is at present to be sought at a significantly higher level than the essential nature of the plant – in other words, that we cannot find a 'type' for the ego corresponding to the archetypal plant – we can conceive, nevertheless, that in humanity's evolution the 'I', too, has been received from without, from the spiritual world, and that all human egos consist of a common archetypal substance that comes from the realm of the sun gods who sacrificed part of their ego nature to human beings. Thus the 'I' was bequeathed by beings of the hierarchy of the exusiai to still slumbering human souls, the archetypal impulse of love necessary for this emanating from the greatest of sun beings, the Christ Logos. In this sense we can say that later on, in Christ Jesus, the divine archetypal image of the human 'I' descended to earth. 'In the human being who bears the name of Christ live also the forces of the exalted sun being in which every human "I" had its origin.'[46]

Thus, insofar as we remain conscious of the different spiritual levels between them, we can say that in the same way as we look at the archetypal plant in order to understand the form of a plant, asking how the archetypal plant lives in a specific plant form, so, to understand the essential nature of a human being, we can look to the Christ and try to see the human 'I' in the rays of the Christ light.

Put like this, it certainly sounds very abstract still, and does not yet awaken any idea of how we might realize this in practice. Yet as a practical aid for cultivating this kind of understanding, Rudolf Steiner gave us the statue of the 'Representative of Humanity'. This depicts the active power of the Christ as He battles to re-establish humanity's fallen and partially lost figure as it was originally formed in the image of God. Just as we can use 'perceiving powers of judgement' (Goethe) to 'perceivingly think' and 'thinkingly perceive' the archetypal plant in every plant derived from it, so, with the help of thoughts uplifted by reverence and love, we can sense in every human 'I' the far-reaching yet also intimate presence of the Christ 'I', the divine representative of humankind, which, though living in the here and now, encompasses both past and future. Christ is there for us, suffering for us, continuously overshadowed by dark clouds, continuously exposed to death, yet also continuously overcoming it, weaving together heavenly dimensions and earthly destiny. In every human 'I' lives this relationship to Christ – our original potential for the sun-radiant, magnanimous power of benevolence, even though often only in hidden, germinal form. In every human being this innate desire must mature and develop in us to ever greater independence through confrontation with adversarial powers. And in every human being Christ is there, to battle alongside us. We can become aware of this divine presence as soon as we break through the undergrowth of fixed, rigidified judgements about another for a moment ('he is noble, clever and skilful', 'he is lazy, vain and coarse ...'), thus entering the stream of living thoughts. The adversary powers infiltrate the soul life of all of us, but not only in a negative sense, for our 'I' can gain many qualities from them that we need to be able to work at transforming the earth in freedom. Lucifer is not only a seducer who inflames our human passions; he also kindles enthusiasm, imagination and contemplative humour. And Ahriman is not only the imperious dictator who chains human beings to the sense world, and the prince of death; humanity also gains clarity in thinking from him, logical consistency, inner resilience and steadfastness. What we get from the Christ is the strength to gradually transform the evil aspects of the two adversaries into good and helpful qualities.

Imagine a human being standing in front of you. His present form of soul and spirit has been acquired through his previous development, with the help of a great many influences from his surroundings. But he is not only the person we see and hear before us. The kind of thinking that lives in dynamic movement shows him, as every other person, to be an individual elaboration of the motif captured in the statue of the 'Representative of Humanity:' Christ confronting and engaging with Lucifer and Ahriman. In a particular case it may be that Christ can only work upon a person's 'I' from, as it were, a great distance. It may also be the case that Lucifer and Ahriman predominate in him and tempt him to evil. But if, nevertheless, we succeed in using imaginative thought, even if very imperfectly, to grasp the interplay of the three powers in the specific form they have assumed in this particular person, then Lucifer and Ahriman will quite certainly cease to reveal only their adversarial forces, and it will become apparent how many positive qualities might also be won from them. The first tender rays of future promise begin to dawn around the person, so that the way we see him is permeated by Christ.

We can embark on the path towards this kind of imaginative experience of another by starting to ask calm questions imbued with feelings of reverence and love, such as: In what sort of situations in life does this person show something of a Christ potential? Where, at all, in what kind of remarks – positive or negative – does a luciferic element appear? In what way does Ahriman appear to work in him? The goal of these efforts is this kind of imaginative experience – based of course on us having absorbed some sense of the significance of time in human life, as we endeavoured to describe it.

Immediately after the first world war, when Rudolf Steiner witnessed the collapse of all social cohesion amongst the people of Europe, he showed extraordinary vehemence and energy in addressing his audience on ways of nurturing new social community. At the time he spoke the following words, which can sum up and round off the thoughts we have presented here about observing human beings in a living and life-enhancing way:

'My dear friends, you can look at an image such as that depicted in the sculptural group of the Representative of Humanity with Lucifer and Ahriman. Here, for the first time, you see before you something that works within the whole human being, for each person is a point of balance between luciferic and ahrimanic forces. *Fill your life with the impulse to meet each human being in such a way that you see this trinity in him, really see it, then you will begin to understand him.* And this is an essential power that must develop in the fifth post-Atlantean period: no longer to pass one another by, like ghosts, forming no picture of each other, merely defining each other in abstract concepts. That is really all we do now. We pass one another by like ghosts, thinking: That is a nice fellow, but that one isn't so nice; this one is a bad person and that one a good person. We use nothing but abstract concepts in such judgements. Our social exchanges are nothing but a bundle of abstract concepts. This is where the Old Testament commandment "Make no image" can ultimately lead us: to anti-social forces, if we continue in this way. What emanates from our inner being, striving to be realized, is that an image arises when one person meets another, arises as it were out of the other person: a picture of the particular state of equilibrium which each person individually expresses. This of course involves that heightened interest I have often described to you as being the foundation for social life: the heightened interest which one human being should feel for another. Today, our interest in other people is not yet keen enough. This is why we criticize them, judge them or form opinions according to our sympathies and antipathies and not according to the objective picture that springs to meet us from the other person.

'Now, my dear friends, you might ask how we can gradually become able to allow the picture of another person to rise towards us. We have to learn this through life... If we look back in a more selfless way at what we experienced in childhood, youth and so on, depending on the age we are now, there appear to us, as though rising from hazy depths of spirit, various people who participated in our lives in all sorts of different ways. Look back on your life, my dear friends, but focus less on what is so special and interesting about you yourself, and more on the figures who approached you, teaching you something, making friends with you, helping you, or even harming you – sometimes even harming you in a very useful way. Something will then dawn on you, my dear friends: how little, when it comes to it, people have reason to attribute to themselves what they have become… Once people really look at themselves in the way I have just described, they will find themselves far too uninteresting to want to brood on their own lives very much. Endless light is shed on our lives once we see them illumined by what comes to meet us from these grey, hazy depths.

'This, however, enriches us so that we acquire the kind of imaginative forces to meet people in our present lives in a way that allows us to perceive in them, now, what otherwise we would only see years later by looking back on those we were once connected with. By doing this we acquire the capacity to perceive pictures rising towards us from the people we meet…

'But when we can form a *picture* of our fellow human being, we enrich our soul life; with every person we get to know, our inner soul life acquires a treasure. We make it possible for the other person to live in us. But this is an acquired capacity; we are not born with it.'[47]

In our presentation of living thinking we have now, in considering the human being, arrived at the third level of thought training. As we mentioned already (page 58), once we grasp that at this level concepts are infused with and emanate a moral dimension, we can increasingly experience thoughts as *living beings*. Here we will briefly suggest how this living quality of thought can also be inwardly perceived and observed. We will see that the concepts which have been awoken into a certain mobility are all of a sudden much more difficult to express in words. And we will also discover the reason for this: it is due to the fact that in modern languages over the past few centuries nouns have disproportionately increased in importance, whilst other parts of speech are often inserted between the nouns merely as connecting and less intrinsically significant parts of speech. Nouns in particular are ideal for conveying sharply outlined concepts, since their meaning can usually be easily and clearly defined. In the service of modern, more or less abstract scientific thinking, nouns have become the bearers of unambiguous, definite and therefore rigid and dead concepts. Even our sense of the original content of a noun such as 'movement' has almost been lost: it now largely conveys only a schematic, expressionless 'something,' that one could just as well express in a formula or diagram. How differently we are affected still by words such as 'mobile', 'lively' or 'active', or even more so by the verbal phrase 'it is moving'. Here we suddenly encounter a meaning that is not fixed, not enclosed in abstract stasis, but contains an unlimited continuity. Whilst nouns supply us with a clear orientation among the things of our physical environment, verbs arise from the flowing, transforming condition of the archetypes in 'spirit land'. But as we are used to thinking in nouns, we have difficulties in understanding as soon as we have to express the flowing life of higher reality.

Rudolf Steiner often speaks of nouns as not being a suitable means of communication when contacting beings of the spiritual world. The dead hardly understand us if we send them thoughts expressed in nouns:

'And if we examine this whole matter more closely, we find that verbs especially, prepositions too, and above all interjections, can fairly easily be understood by the dead, whereas they hardly understand nouns at all. Nouns form so to speak a kind of gap in their understanding of language. The dead fail to understand you if you use too many nouns. But they will start to if you try to change a noun into a verb. If, for instance, you say to the soul of a dead person: "The germ of something…" – then in most cases the word "germ" is not understood; in fact it is as though the soul heard nothing at all. But if you say: "It is germinating" – that is, if you change "the germ" into the verbal phrase "it is germinating" – he begins to understand.'[48]

An extraordinarily helpful exercise for developing sense-free thinking is to think as clearly as possible about the difference between various word categories: verbal forms are the natural form of expression for 'mobile', 'living' concepts. While nouns correspond primarily to abstract head thinking, verbs, which usually express activity, address the will sphere – that is, the aspect of us that also moves our body. By thinking in verbs, therefore, we can in a sense prefigure from the realm of 'pure thinking' what is experienced at the third level on the path of thinking.

The difference between the two stages lies in the fact that although thinking in verbal forms allows us to experience a will quality, we still have an unclear, or at best shadowy awareness of the moral aspect of concepts. On the other hand, at the third level we begin to feel our way into the hidden moral tendencies of concepts that are enlivened into thought beings. It is this that increasingly gives concepts – or thoughts – real independence as living beings. They reveal themselves to us more or less clearly, as morally endowed beings.

This experience of thinking, radically alters – though only at rare, festive moments in which we elevate ourselves to it – the nature of our thought activity, and the way we connect or separate thoughts. We become aware that logical compulsion in the way we link thoughts grows ever weaker. The laws of logic do not lose their validity but they do diminish in importance. We become freer in our thinking. Thoughts, through their own intrinsic nature and being, through what we have described as their moral content, reveal their mutual similarity or dissimilarity, whether they relate to one another or repel one another, feel drawn to each other or avoid each other. And when we think, we simply follow these tendencies in a loving way; we endeavour to think in harmony with the spiritual, moral lawfulness that manifests in thoughts themselves. So long as we remember that our thought connections may only arise through active thinking effort and consequently have nothing to do with passive thought association, we can go so far as to say: We let our thoughts think themselves. Rudolf Steiner expresses it like this:

'By making what spiritual research offers us increasingly our own we accustom ourselves to a mode of thinking which does not draw its contents from sense observations. We learn to recognize how, in the inner reaches of the soul, thought weaves into thought, how thought seeks thought, although the thought connections are not instigated by the power of sensory observation. The essential thing here is that we become aware of how our thought world has an inner life, of how, by really thinking, we already find ourselves in the region of a living, supersensible world... In order to see correctly in this regard we must be able to have the following inner experience. We must learn to distinguish between thought associations which we create arbitrarily, and those which we experience within us when we silence this arbitrary volition. In the latter case I can then say: I remain quite silent within myself; I create no thought associations; I surrender myself to what "thinks in me". I am then fully justified in saying: Something possessing the nature of real being works in me...' [49]

Once one has found a way in to such experiences, one acquires greater respect for the way in which, in books, thoughts are linked to thoughts; whether a particular author is capable of hearing the direction a particular thought is seeking to take, or whether he forcefully compels thoughts to obey his intentions. By experiencing thoughts more and more as real, our capacity to perceive purely logical connections also becomes sharper. And we also become aware of how respectfully and carefully Rudolf Steiner handled his thoughts. If we can notice in his philosophical writings how, understandably, he prioritized absolutely devoted observance of logical consistency, we shall notice and repeatedly admire in his later writings, and especially lectures, that strict attention to the *actual inner character of thoughts* we have been describing. This attentiveness also involved not fundamentally altering the angle from which he approached certain facts, even if, due to such 'disciplined onesidedness', apparent contradictions arose now and again with other remarks of his. What Steiner does is allow his thoughts to form connections according to their own intrinsic nature. And his realism remains faithful as demonstrated by the fact that circumstances described from various angles sometimes inevitably had to be expressed in contradictory ways.

Seven

The Fourth Level: Sacrifice

Do we make it clear to ourselves sufficiently often that each person has a different kind of experience of the world, and therefore a different understanding of it? Is this simply because everyone's experience of the world is based on different inner preconditions?

'Some people sail across the ocean but have little inner experience of it; others, on the same journey, hear the eternal language of the cosmic spirit unveiling to them the mysteries of existence... The outer world, with all its phenomena, is filled with divine splendour, but we must have experienced the divine within ourselves before we can hope to discover it in our surroundings.' [50]

The wealth of our inner life forms the key to a wealth of knowledge of the universe. How different each person's inner life is! How difficult this makes it for us to understand one another! Yet, in our thinking we have the objective, connecting thread that can link one soul to another. But we have seen that even the actual content of a person's concepts depends on the way their inner being participates in their thinking process. Mutual understanding is actually comparatively easy only at the level of intellectual head thinking. If we experience a thought, and this thought is sufficiently clearly defined, every other person should be able to understand us, for in this case all of us can repeat exactly the same connecting of concepts. Although our concepts are shadowy they are more or less common to all of us.

This changes as soon as we leave the 'head' level. Now, the content of our concepts is no longer the same for everyone. How, indeed, should anyone who thinks only with his intellect be able to comprehend the thoughts of someone who forms them with reverence? The further removed we get from ordinary abstract thinking the more alone we are in our knowledge. 'Those who pilgrimage towards truth, journey alone'. (Christian Morgenstern). But even two people who both absorb anthroposophical insights with reverence do not think in the same concepts, for each of them will have his or her own personal way of infusing his thoughts with wonder, veneration and devotion. Even when thinking an angel, each individual will have a different vividness or vivacity, a different kind of intimacy with reality.

This applies quite particularly to what we called the third stage, where our thoughts are infused with Michaelic warmth. Here an endless horizon of diverse possibilities opens up for grasping the hidden moral world order in human thoughts; also an endless series of steps in maturity in relation to our efforts. Just think of all that is required to be able to include at all in one's small, human-sized world picture, even as an inkling, the sacrificial will of the Thrones at the world's beginning! Only when the most humble reverence, coupled with our own capacity to love and make sacrifices, has helped shape and form the vessel of knowledge, is there a hope of such truths being received and continuing to live in our soul. People come to study anthroposophy by different paths of destiny, and each will bring with him the most diverse moral foundations for understanding great cosmic facts. Let us also not forget that any such understanding will still be human and thus inadequate, and will pale in comparison with the grandeur of spiritual realities. A purely intellectual grasp of the circumstances of the world's creation, on the other hand, as conveyed to us by anthroposophy, does not appear so difficult at all. People unwilling to make sacrifices in life, to be there for others in an unselfish way, can scarcely have anything more than the most imperfect understanding of the world's creation as Steiner describes it, and will likewise find it very hard to comprehend the idea of a moral world order inherent in the visible cosmos. The idea of a 'big bang' as explanation of the world's origins may well satisfy them, in contrast, since that is something they can fully understand.

To grow ever more consciously with our view of the world into the unfathomable, fiery depths of the divine order of love that permeates the cosmos, we need to work tirelessly and faithfully to develop moral qualities that can deepen our knowledge. We gradually have to form in ourselves, however modestly, a picture of the morality that courses through the cosmos, even though natural human weaknesses will invariably accompany our efforts. So much is involved in this statement! Only think for instance of how the life of the whole universe comes into being and passes away solely through the all-governing cycle of sacrificial surrender: the most sublime beings give up part of their own being to allow for other beings to arise, and these repeat this act of sacrifice through which they received their own existence as a gift. Ever more numerous beings are awoken into existence to participate in the hierarchies' sacrificial hymn resounding throughout the cosmos, descending from the heights and penetrating ever further into the depths, until a world of innumerable created beings rejoice in existence. And when cosmic life has come full circle, passing through seed form, germinating, blossoming and ripening, the last of the created beings give themselves back in exuberant gratefulness to their creators, merge with them, with all that they possess; these beings then give themselves to those next above them, and these in turn to still loftier ones – right up to the prime creators of the cosmos – until ultimately everything has merged with primal, divine substance and a cosmic aeon closes, so that a new aeon can awaken into existence. How could we really 'understand' even single details of such divine, spiritual lawfulness, were it not for our own inner awareness of a quiet yearning to participate also in this sublime, life-creating, sacrificial act; to join in, ourselves, in this hymn of love resounding from the love of the hierarchies.

To wonder and reverence, as the first prerequisites for knowledge truly responsive to reality, Rudolf Steiner adds two further, even loftier conditions. The first of these is: *'feeling oneself in wise harmony with cosmic laws'*. [51] Something similar is also expressed in the words of the final part of the liturgy of The Christian Community, which speaks of a 'peaceful relation to the world' and of 'uniting with its unfolding'. We cannot understand the real, primal foundations of the world unless we seek to be in *harmony* with its morality, to recognize the laws of its existence and allow these to work in us. Not until we voluntarily unite through love with these cosmic laws themselves can we reach the point when the world begins to reveal to us its deeper, moral content. Only then can thoughts be experienced as living realities that whisper their hidden secrets to human beings.

But we should clearly realize that even then, having worked persistently and humbly to acquire knowledge, our efforts to understand will still contain an echo of the fall of man.

Even if we do not try to 'seize hold' of knowledge any more, even though we refashion our thoughts into receiving vessels and patiently accept whether an answer is granted to us or not, whether we succeed or not in our attempt to penetrate a spiritual-scientific matter with understanding, our efforts still remain a gift of Lucifer. If human beings had not allied themselves to Lucifer they would have become 'beings whose conscious knowledge would not have reflected the cosmos in pictures created by their own free volition but as a necessity of nature'. [52] Every conscious striving for knowledge is a kind of continuation of the fall of man, even if it is also the only way to overcome it. Without this 'fall,' human beings would have received all their knowledge without engaging their will, merely passively accepting it; they would never have had to exert themselves to reach it, for, without having to lift a finger, so to speak, they would have been filled continually with true thoughts; and they would have had no possibility of doing wrong, for the kind of knowledge they needed at any given moment would have always been readily available.

As long as we engage actively with knowledge, as long as we yearn to attain a particular insight, to reach a certain goal in our understanding, then the fall cannot be redeemed in our life of cognition. Even though Lucifer can lead us in knowledge as far as the Christ (as we saw in relation to the third stage) the former still remains at our side, accompanying us. Would it be better to renounce all knowledge? Or is there perhaps a kind of knowledge, in conjunction with which we remain fully conscious, yet contribute no activity to acquiring it?

Rudolf Steiner gives the following condition as the final, momentous and most difficult of all the conditions for a form of knowledge imbued with reality: '*Submission to the world process*'.

He says in this connection that we should work at self-development until we reach the point where truth streams into and pervades us as revelation of all things. Then we perceive 'the will in the world'.

How does a kind of knowledge arise that comes from practising 'submission to the world process'? Here it is no longer only a matter of including feeling or will in our efforts to gain knowledge. Now we have to gain insight without exerting our will, for clearly, 'exerting our will to achieve it' does not coincide with 'submission'. To put it more bluntly: here we need to think without wanting to grasp anything by doing so. Is this possible? It is no doubt comprehensible that such a stance would indeed signify a reversal of the fall in relation to knowledge. Can we assume, however, that knowledge will stream towards us if we do not even go in search of it? Of course, a kind of knowledge exists which people receive involuntarily, will-lessly: for instance in trance-like states. Yet this is the sort of knowledge whose actual source can hardly be traced, and whose truth is uncertain to start with and usually defies any penetration by thought. Really knowing something cannot be a matter of 'submitting' in the sense of giving up one's alert, waking consciousness. The path we are pursuing to transform thinking activity cannot end in a denial of thinking.

So how do we realize this challenge to 'submit to the world process' with alert thinking? There is in fact a special mode of thinking which does not set out to grasp or ascertain anything with willed intention, or set any aims of acquiring knowledge, but can still grant us fresh insights. This is *meditation*, in which you study a certain thought, but not in order to learn something through thinking, not to discover new connections or contexts of thought. Withdrawing from everything else, we give ourselves up to a single thought, concentrate wholly on it, allowing it to speak to us in reverent, loving sincerity – and initially nothing more than this. We do not expect to be rewarded for our trouble, but just rejoice in this one thought. We are not seeking to acquire further knowledge. But as the thought becomes more and more spiritually real through meditating on it, it can, under certain circumstances, eventually become a door into the supersensible world, mediating spiritual revelations. These are revelations, mark you, that are not striven or longed for, but which descend from the spiritual world as a gift of grace, as a gratifying answer to an effort of thought not aimed at any kind of achieved insight.

Meditation thus arises from renunciation, from sacrifice of knowledge, the absence of a wish to know in the earthly-human sense. It is therefore a thought activity that wrests reasoning human beings from the domain of sin and returns them to their original, divine calling. Thinking here ceases to be used as a means to understand the world, and is transformed into a purely sacrificial activity, a *self-surrender*. In this kind of thinking, we give ourselves in reverence and love to the spiritual world. This brings us to *the fourth stage, the highest stage of the Michaelic path of thinking.*

Precisely because, at this stage, we offer up our thinking as a sacrifice, we can feel ourselves in thinking harmony with the spiritual world. A ray streaming from humanity's heavenly future touches us, an inkling of humanity's entry into the sacrificial dance of divine creator beings:

'Surrendering to the all-governing sway of the cosmic existence surrounding us, we can live in what we perform as transubstantiation within the great temple of the cosmos, standing within it purely spiritually in a sacrificial capacity. What would otherwise be merely abstract knowledge becomes a relationship of feeling and will to the world. The world becomes a temple, the world becomes a house of God. Human beings, in their capacity to know, bestirring themselves in feeling and will, become beings capable of sacrifice. Human beings' fundamental relationship to the world rises from perception and knowledge of the world to cosmic worship.' [53]

In this renunciation of knowledge, which can become a portal to higher knowing, thinking attains the goal of its human mission. It has made human beings into individual, free 'I's; and now it returns them to the spirit world. Through Lucifer, human beings came to themselves. Through Lucifer, however, they can also be led as thinkers to the Christ. And the nearer they come to their goal, the more clearly do they know that Christ accompanied them from the very beginning, and that Lucifer has increasingly become Christ's helper. Lucifer is increasingly receding as the one who endows us with our sense of self, is less and less the proud prince of self-glorification. And finally, at the last stage of thinking's transformation, where knowledge is sacrificed, he disappears completely, and the Christ alone stands before human beings as high priest of the earth aeon, offering Himself continuously in sacrificial atonement on humanity's behalf until we grow mature enough to give ourselves in self-surrender. In finding the Christ, human beings find in Him and through Him their lost access to the jubilant, divine worship of angel choirs. 'Anthroposophy is a path of knowledge leading the spiritual in the human being to the spiritual in the universe'. [54] And by surrendering thinking to the spiritual cosmos, and thus, at the threshold to higher worlds, allowing this thinking to stream back into the Michael sphere, anthroposophy too can see its earthly mission moving towards fulfilment. To the words we have already quoted, Rudolf Steiner adds the following: 'The first beginning of what has to happen if anthroposophy is to accomplish its mission in the world is found where we perceive our whole relation to the world as a cosmic rite of worship.'[55]

What can be accomplished and experienced in this way at the fourth stage of deepened thinking is what Steiner calls the 'spiritual communion of humanity'. We did, of course, quote similar words at the end of the chapter on the 'first stage,' which concerned sense-free thinking – words which he wrote in the period before his work in spiritual science began: 'Becoming aware how the idea lives in reality is true human communion'. True communion thus means 'becoming one' with spirit. This was the fruit of Steiner's spiritual disclosures at that period. He was showing us that the spirit was not something in the 'beyond' or 'unfathomable', something incomprehensible, but something that can be experienced in thinking by actually observing thinking. Already at that period of his life, therefore, he was giving the spirit back to humanity in a new form.

But we also saw what a long journey it was from that simple first level of encountering the spirit right through to a devotional immersion in the spirit world. Pure thoughts had first of all to be formed into reverential vessels to receive cosmic facts. Then they had to become vessels of love, to be able to hold the first inklings of the moral world order. Finally they had to become sacrificial vessels so that human beings could participate, in deep contemplation, in the sacrificial hymns of the heavenly hosts. But here, at this ultimate stage, where human beings not only 'think' but surrender their human nature in thought, the word 'spiritual communion' recurs once more. The same word, yet with an altered, spiritually transfigured meaning. It is now different, weightier, much more responsible than before. We hear, now, that communion in spirit is the highest achievement attainable by us on earth, a prefiguring of the earth's ultimate goal, a fulfilment of divine purposes, an experience of Lucifer's eventual transformation and his re-uniting with Christ. What a wealth of possibilities unfold for us as we strive for knowledge!

Yet all of this is already present as seed in the experience we undergo at the first level. The first time Steiner wrote down the words about communion in the realm of ideas, they were already founded on his own wholly valid experience, signifying for him a possible means of access to all the heights and depths of the spirit – and not only for him personally. In writing down these words they became a promise to all those who would read them and wish to prove them true. As soon as we realize that, in the idea, we contact the creative spirit of the cosmos, we already stand before an open door, and have even already embarked on the path. Nothing prevents us entering the spirit world. It is like getting to know another person: initially we know next to nothing about them, but an opportunity exists to become ever better acquainted.

Already at the first stage, therefore, we can experience the spirit as spirit. And spiritual communion becomes more profound and rich from stage to stage. One experiences ever more profound layers of spiritual reality, is led 'from one level of clarity to another', as Paul says. At the first stage one experiences the first caress of the spirit. At the last stage one actually enters the all-governing life of the divine world. Rudolf Steiner discovered all these stages by arduous effort, and showed us the way to achieve them. They form the new current of thinking, part of the path of knowledge which can 'lead the spirit in the human being to the spirit in the universe'.

'All the thoughts we construct for ourselves in ordinary, death-related science are mirror images and not realities. The thoughts we receive from spiritual research are enlivened in imagination, inspiration and intuition. If we receive them they become forms with autonomous existence in earthly life.

'I once said the following about such creative thoughts: This kind of thinking embodies the spiritual form of humanity's capacity to communicate. When people give themselves up to their reflections on external nature they merely repeat the past, and dwell within corpses of the divine. But when they themselves enliven their thoughts, they connect their own being – communicate with, receive communion from – the divine, spiritual powers that permeate the world and assure its future.

'Spiritual knowledge is real communion, the beginning of a cosmic rite and worship appropriate for contemporary humanity.' [56]

Eight

Conclusion: Some Consequences

A while back there was some debate as to whether there is such a thing as an 'anthroposophical picture of the human being.' If we understand by this a single human type, and the obligation to comply with this ideal type, we can answer 'No' without the slightest hesitation, and back this up by adding that the idea of a prefabricated ideal to be aspired to is not compatible with the principle of inner freedom. Anthroposophy is of course addressed exclusively to free individuals: each person can pursue it in an individual manner, work on it in their psyche and assimilate it in their own personal way. There is no reason why we should not maintain and preserve our own characteristic individuality despite living our way into anthroposophy. One might even say that the more seriously we become preoccupied with it the more individual our approach to it will be.

As a specific example let us take various possible ways of approaching the concept 'etheric body' that we come across when reading the book *Theosophy*. One way of acquiring the concept is possibly by simply 'believing' in its existence in the way it is described in this book. No one should be blamed for such an approach, but we ought also to consider that in this case the concept will remain very shadowy and hardly of any use.

Another possibility – as suggested in the introduction to *Theosophy* – would be to examine our own feeling for truth: we can do so, perhaps, by trying to hold onto the mood invoked by the thought that we have an invisible, life-determining member of our being, and enquiring into the dignity and beauty of such a feeling; this is also a possible approach.

Or we could follow another suggestion contained in the introduction to *Theosophy*, namely: 'Ask yourself whether a satisfactory explanation of life is offered if the things stated here are true. You will find that each person's life provides confirmation of them'. In accordance with this guideline we can reflect on life and death as we have so far known them, and ask whether the concept of an etheric body contributes in any way to their understanding. And this will probably result in the concept of an etheric body becoming somewhat more comprehensible.

We can also observe and examine the activity that goes on in our etheric body when our physical body is damaged – the way an injury heals: a broken bone, or wounds following surgery. Those who are disposed to follow clear trains of thought will try to acquire as clear a concept as they can of the etheric body; and they may try to gain insight into life processes – the synthesis and break-down of cells, the mutual dependency of various organ functions, possibly even the rhythmic temporal sequences of life processes. Thinking along these lines will bring them more diverse and specific ideas about how the etheric body works – and also, of course, many new questions to solve, of benefit in their further striving for knowledge.

But of course there is a quite different way to proceed: by studying what else spiritual science says about the etheric body, collecting and compiling these descriptions, and forming for oneself a more comprehensive and substantial idea of it. One can understandably gain more from doing this than from all the

CONCLUSION: SOME CONSEQUENCES

other approaches. You will discover, for instance, that the etheric body incarnates only gradually in children, and that the forces that form their organs change later on into the ability to think; and it may be that our own involvement with children's upbringing or education will give us the chance to test the practical value of assuming the existence of an etheric body.

Many other possible ways of studying the etheric will arise if we consider it as the bearer of memory, or as the seat of the temperaments. We can say in general that many different approaches can be employed to understand any anthroposophical concept; none of these can be prescribed, and each of them can be pursued in an individual way, in an entirely personal life situation, based on personal inclinations and experiences.

Is it conceivable that any of these approaches might have a decisive effect on a person's individual way of expressing himself, on his character, his temperament, his lifelong habits and so on? Or, to be more precise: could they – consciously or unconsciously – impel him closer towards a universal human ideal? Certainly not. People who concern themselves with anthroposophy remain themselves in the deepest sense. Their consciousness of being free cannot be impaired; only, at most, strengthened.

Yet we can ask about an 'anthroposophical picture of the human being' from a different point of view, and by doing so come to an entirely different conclusion. Anthroposophy is certainly not in the first place a world view, a system of concepts, but first and foremost a path: 'A path of knowledge leading the spiritual in the human being to the spiritual in the universe'. To connect with anthroposophy means more than acquiring certain concepts; it means *to embark on a particular path*. You are of course free; free to limit yourself to occupying yourself *solely* with anthroposophical *thoughts*, and can even do this by testing them in life with thorough honesty, actually applying them; and you can, indeed, accept everything Steiner says in perfectly good faith, and even also become a member of the Anthroposophical Society; yet despite all this you will still not be, in the real sense of the word, an anthroposophist. How do you become an anthroposophist? Anthroposophy is a path, which means it is movement; and sometimes this expresses itself as really tumultuous inner movement. To connect with anthroposophy means to connect with this real dynamic. Just think for a moment of the aspect of this movement dynamic discussed in this book: the inner path by means of which feeling and will become powers of cognition. This alone signifies a radical change in the way we relate to the world, a drastic transformation of our soul life. And we can never really understand anthroposophy as a path of development if we remain a spectator on the margins. We cannot fully understand anthroposophy without seeking to realize it in ourselves. This is not to say that as an anthroposophist we should immediately manifest certain results of higher knowledge, for instance the capacity for imagination, inspiration and intuition. The path certainly does not begin with such results. And we do not even have to strive for them consciously. The path usually begins very inconspicuously, possibly by reading a particular book that gives you a sense that the person you are at present is not quite equal to anthroposophical thoughts. You feel drawn to them, but at the same time you notice that you cannot quite inhabit them, that – for whatever reason – you remain outside. So you make up your mind to give greater attention to them. And this decision in itself is the first, gentle beginning of really working on yourself, embarking on a path – which happens almost without you noticing. This embarking on the path can obviously happen in all sorts of individually different ways. The same is true of the moment at which people begin to pursue the path *consciously*, which will be when they ask themselves: 'How should I set about working on myself?' What is important is that in deciding to take up anthroposophy one is necessarily committing one self to pursuing a *path*.

Let us return to the example of the etheric body. The reader may have noticed that the approaches so far described in this chapter – for going beyond a mere reading of *Theosophy* and seeking ways to acquire greater clarity about the etheric body – are not the same as the path to which this book is dedicated. The reader may also have noticed that all the concepts thus acquired ultimately remain in the sphere of the intellect, the head sphere. Initially there is nothing wrong with that, for in most cases absorbing anthroposophy through thinking tends to begin more or less with this sort of intellectual questioning – during which people probably realize that anthroposophy supplies a more useful world view, even in intellectual terms, than the orthodox sciences. Yet the concept of the etheric body gained in this way will lack something very important: life itself. It remains immobile, inflexible, unreceptive to further aspects, above all not really receptive to the fundamental aspect of time at work in the activity of life forces – which comes to clear expression in *Theosophy*: the etheric body as the force underlying growth and reproduction. It is precisely this aspect of time that should give readers of *Theosophy* the chance to notice that at this point the ordinary concepts they make use of are entirely inadequate for grasping the phenomenon of a process of development, of change through time. So they should now, in fact, pause and feel a momentary sensation of powerlessness that overcomes their thinking, and both the need and importance of entering into a deeply-grounded new world of thoughts. At this moment a breath of reverence for this unknown thought world ought to waft through their inner being and touch their thinking, at first perhaps bringing a sense of insecurity. Yet this reverence can stimulate them to try to form clearer, more pictorial ideas about growth, that is, about the whole, endlessly repeating cycle from seed through the fully developed plant to the seed again. By doing so, the concept of the etheric body will start to acquire a first hint of mobility. And if readers of *Theosophy* wish to pursue this path energetically they will be led, by the intrinsic logic of the matter itself, to study Goethe's concept of type, for example; or they will think about the development, consistency, form and function of their own various inner organs, and in this connection encounter the anthroposophical idea that the etheric body is a mediator of different planetary influences. And then they will suddenly discover the mysterious connections of the human organism with the cosmos. This ought to bring them 'as though of itself' to the reverential level of thinking, and through this to the realm of 'Michaelic' thinking. People are free at any moment to cease pursuing this. But ongoing progress in anthroposophy, insofar as this is undertaken seriously and honestly, will stimulate people to work ever further at transforming themselves. Anthroposophy is a path, and anthroposophy will change people increasingly into inwardly homeless pilgrims, so that they may seek and find their spiritual home.

This, of course, already relates to a 'picture of the human being' – a first, shared characteristic of all human beings who connect with the essential being of anthroposophy. But 'being on a path' is not something to which only anthroposophists can lay claim, for there are, of course, a great many people of different spiritual persuasions who work with dedication at their inner development. What exclusively distinguishes anthroposophy is the fact that it is a path of *knowledge*. The inner progress we strive for and undergo as anthroposophists therefore, expresses itself in the first place in our cognitive life. Our example was intended to show that in coming to grips with anthroposophical accounts – simply by desiring to know – we quite naturally arrive at the point of developing new qualities in our thinking. This effort of thinking ought in the first place to lead to the level of *pure thinking*. But this does not always happen, or not always consciously, and not always consistently. So although the capacity to think in a sense-free way could be acknowledged as a further characteristic of an 'anthroposophical picture of the human being,' it is not always acquired, and cannot, either, be easily recognized in the way people express their thoughts. It is more a soul quality, which is hardly seen outwardly or in social interaction. When we speak of an image or picture of the human being, by contrast, we instinctively mean something that we can also recognize externally. For these reasons we would probably not include the capacity for pure thinking in the 'anthroposophical picture of the human being'.

It is different when we come to the second level of spiritualizing thinking. *Filling thinking with reverence* is an eminently social aspect of soul life; at least it should change the way people behave towards their fellow human beings. And we can see this, too, in the way people communicate, the way they connect one thought with another, and the way they express themselves. We could therefore say that this capacity might be the determining characteristic of an 'anthroposophical picture of the human being'. This does not mean that this capacity immediately makes people appear different. Here too it is a matter of very subtle new characteristics. At first this transformation in thinking does not affect people's temperament to the slightest degree; the most that happens is that we can count on their character acquiring a new accent or emphasis, which also indicates they are on an inner path, have embarked on self-development. Such a change ought to be apparent to a discriminating, perceptive faculty of thinking. It should therefore be *the first characteristic common to all anthroposophists.*

The first common characteristic: so is there, after all, a generally valid 'anthroposophical picture of the human being'? In this sense – yes, there is. Does this mean therefore that anthroposophists are not entirely 'free' human beings? No: they *are* free. We have to remember that they do not imbue their thoughts with reverence because this is an ideal externally imposed on them. All they desire is to fill their understanding with spiritual content; and transforming their thinking is the necessary means to this. Doing so means they lose their freedom just as little as someone who uses a hammer to knock a nail into a wall. Similarly, all the advice in *Knowledge of the Higher Worlds*, which could well be considered 'moralizing,' is certainly not a prescription with the goal of achieving particular moral ideals; by no means are they moral norms, but solely an indication that essential things can be done to enliven spiritual organs of perception. Obviously, in following these indications, anthroposophists add certain characteristic features to their own embodiment of the 'picture of the human being'; and they do this all the more clearly the longer they work at them. But this restricts their freedom just as little as developing human love or human understanding. On the anthroposophical path of schooling we can also acquire general virtues and inner capacities that not only do not interfere with inner freedom but which in the truest sense of the word actually provide the basis for it: they ease compulsions, resolve dependencies, and free the way for our 'inner ruler' to hold sway, our individual 'I'. They are therefore characteristic features of a really free human being. And the same applies to the quality of reverence-filled thinking.

Yet – do anthroposophists really have this quality? Are there really people who have it? Certainly there are such people; they are to be found, for instance, among anthroposophical teachers, or co-workers in village communities for children and young people with special needs; that is, among people whose particular professional work helps them judge those around them less critically and more positively. It is understandable that positivity is extremely beneficial for developing forces of reverence. And how does this stage of thinking manifest in other people seriously engaged in anthroposophy? In the first chapter of this book we mentioned that we see far too little awareness of Steiner's legacy in the sense of transformed thinking. And even if there are numerous anthroposophists who 'start from the premise of bringing devotion into their thinking,' this mode of thinking is usually confined to the study of anthroposophical texts. Why?

It does not appear to be an easy matter for the new kind of thinking to build bridges, as it were, from study to actually living with other people. To make this kind of transition from inner to outer work two things are needed: first, the capacity to form our own thoughts reverently, and to remain open to the spirit; and then also the ability, in community with others, to carry these thoughts over into the logical concepts and modes of expression of our modern age. The temptation, each time, is to keep one's own understanding of the world to oneself; to bury it in one's own soul, so to speak, while making use, 'out there', of generally accepted contexts of thought. If we do this, the 'anthroposophical picture of the human being' cannot surface at all and become manifest. Anthroposophy is then shut off from the rest of the human world and loses the opportunity of working in a fruitful, inspiring and therapeutic way on the social environment.

This danger is especially evident in some of the ways in which people stand up for anthroposophy publicly. Here too it is important to adapt the anthroposophical knowledge we acquire with the aid of reverence to the way our listeners think, without – as would be far easier – falling back entirely into the comfortable realm of head thinking, and thus trying to make anthroposophical conclusions plausible to others. Anthroposophy can be presented in such situations as an attractive conceptual system, an advantageous way of looking at and explaining the world, backed up by various historical or other facts, and apparently proven by means of ordinary, intellectual logic. But by doing this you speak to the audience without connecting to the spirit in your own thinking; and those who attend in the hope of finding and being touched by the living spirit depart again unsatisfied. Such an approach has no chance of manifesting the living being of anthroposophy – which invariably is what such occasions require.

The inability to engage our own reverential thoughts in a social context is particularly apparent where there is absolutely no need to adapt them to intellectual, head-focused thinking: in the encounters and disputes of anthroposophists amongst themselves. Are such arguments necessary? Should we have them at all? Well – why not? They can be useful, and can contribute a great deal to clearing up problems that repeatedly surface. Reverence certainly does not exclude criticism. But we should be careful to see that reverence always precedes criticism. To understand Lucifer and Ahriman we have to approach them in the first place with reverential thoughts, for after all they are far superior to us. Not until we realize this is there any sense in our asking when, and in which areas, they hinder human development – after which we can then energetically oppose their influence. As we said, reverence does not exclude criticism. Nor does it require us, on principle, to hide our opinions, or even express ourselves with feigned politeness. What is important, however, is that we do not try to contradict other people's thoughts merely logically, but instead try to experience these thoughts as spiritual reality, as spiritual beings containing much more than abstract, logical, superficial meaning. Understanding is not enhanced if our prime concern is to ask whether these thoughts are logically debatable or not, whether they agree with Steiner's findings, or whether they advance the anthroposophical cause. That sort of thing is of secondary importance. First of all we should ask what kind of spiritual, moral substance these thoughts contain. Are they, in themselves, sound or wholesome thoughts? What new spiritual message do they bring? How do they link up with other thoughts? These are the kinds of questions that require great personal responsibility, and render argument far less vigorous than a strictly logical, generally comprehensible approach. But they do allow us to stay at the level of spiritually open thinking.

And by maintaining spiritual openness in our thinking, we can keep alive in us the sense that every deeper truth anchored in the spirit can only surface in connection with other points of view, especially opposing ones. In this way we can have a spiritual debate with 'our loins girt about with truth'.

Just as the mode of thought that has entered the world with anthroposophy is something new and unfamiliar, even perhaps disorientating, its conscious application in the way we sought to describe here – the exchange of ideas from different points of view in a common search for truth – represents something new and unfamiliar in the history of ideas. One could also characterize the kind of debate or argument that moves in this direction as a modern Christianizing, or anthroposophical recasting, of originally warlike Mars impulses.

On the other hand one might object that this kind of mutual wrestling with ideas embodies a barely realizable ideal. This is true. It is an ideal. But is it not a good thing, now and again, to muse on this kind of distant possibility when we are trying to 'bring anthroposophy into life'?

Now we may also be prompted, in a somewhat different way, to build a bridge for our spirit-filled thoughts to enter the social realm. Besides merely standing up against someone else's opinion, we may also find it necessary to oppose his way of doing things, his actions, which we consider to be wrong. Here it is no longer a matter of thoughts opposing thoughts. We no longer confront someone as thinker but as a person who acts. (We are not thinking now of the innumerable possible blunders that can occur at work or in other areas of outer, practical life, but actions that in some way are expressions of a human personality; in particular the kinds of action where a person intervenes in

CONCLUSION: SOME CONSEQUENCES

anthroposophical life in a particular way, because of his convictions and desire to promote the anthroposophical cause.) What shape will our critical approach take, if we preserve our reverentially-guided thinking?

We need of course to emphasize that when considering such circumstances, prescriptive guidelines for behaviour cannot be involved. A person's behaviour in any particular case must be left entirely to his own freedom. What we need to ask instead is how our thinking can be deepened so that it responds in an entirely free way.

This situation is of course fraught with temptation to enlist ordinary rational logic, for this is by far the most straightforward way of proving that an action is misguided. By doing this, though, you immediately forego your spiritual openness. So from what kind of insights will you draw the impulses which you need for intervening in a potentially critical way?

In chapter 6 we examined how living thinking can transform the way we see others: the possibility of seeing in each person a picture of the Christ battling with Lucifer and Ahriman. If invocation of this picture precedes any criticism it will arouse in us a conscious awareness that criticism has purpose only if it helps the higher 'I' of another to realize itself increasingly in outer actions; that is, if my critical comments help the picture of the Christ to light up more brightly in the other. The most important thing to do, therefore, is not to point out where the other person went 'wrong,' but, through a will to help, to support the other person to find ways of engaging their higher 'I'. Certainly we should not disregard basic, down-to-earth aspects of a situation. However, the kind of thinking strengthened by reverence will hesitate to pillory other people, preferring always to try to connect with the Christ in them without in any way asserting ourselves. Here again, we could speak of a Christianizing of criticism.

Again, we might say that this is an unusual approach to take in arguments with others, seeing it as an ideal very difficult to realize. But such ideals have a very long tradition. Even the Gospels show us two different ways of critically judging another: the criticism of the Pharisees, on the one hand, who always judged any infringement of the law with a feeling of moral superiority; and on the other, the criticism of John the Baptist who, despite radically condemning his contemporaries, does so solely in order to 'prepare the way for the Lord'. Spiritually sincere anthroposophical criticism ought to show the fullest respect for the higher being of the other person, to 'prepare his way'. One might perhaps say that this sort of criticism contains an inkling of an 'anthroposophical picture of the human being'.

To conclude, I should like to attempt at least to hint at the significance of a spiritually attuned transformation of thinking for a person's *fundamental stance of soul* towards the earthly world and contemporary humanity. There are certainly other potential ways of relating to such an underlying outlook, but I want to highlight one that is of special importance to me.

What happens when people meet the world as totality, offering up a vessel to receive knowledge with openness and humility? Rather than their inner relationship to a single phenomenon, my focus here is on all that surrounds them, and their fundamental attitude and feeling. When they do this, what do their vessels of knowledge receive? Actually, this ought really to be the whole spiritual context connected with the earthly world – a bewildering abundance. Yet within this abundant totality one thing shines out brightest of all: the most important, core, significant aspect in the whole spiritual context relating to the earth today. What is this? In other periods it might have been something else, but for contemporary knowledge of the world there is one particular aspect. So what is this key aspect, of the very greatest significance in the whole spiritual dimension of our earth, that distinguishes our age from all past and future ages? It is the descent of the Christ being into the earth's etheric environment, and His activity within it. If we look at the earthly world as the scene of this event, and if we ask to what extent natural processes are receptive and responsive to it – are in a condition to receive it – how must this appear to us?

Surely, what will strike us above all as the most characteristic feature of this century is the endless devastation of all earthly life, the poisoning of the earth, its water and air, the dying and recklessly plundered forests, the extinction of animal species. A great deal is said about this today, and much is being done to save life on earth; and for this we have to be thankful. But our reflections here are not intended to repeat generally accepted ideas about ecological dangers, but rather to stress a quite different aspect: the question of Christ's return. Let us try to see this clearly: on the one hand, Christ approaches amidst a throng of burgeoning life, and on the other He is met by an earth that turns towards Him a polluted, half-dead countenance. But let us examine this more closely: of what do these streams of flowing, burgeoning life consist, in which the Christ is descending to the earth? They are nothing other than a whole summation of many different beings. From the spiritual heights of the sphere of the sun there accompany him various orders of angel beings. In the earth sphere these are joined by spirits of earthly life, countless elemental spirits, the beings who also uninterruptedly sustain organic life on the earth's surface. The ominous global death occurring on the surface of the earth at the same time signifies the disappearance of these all-enlivening, helpful beings. We could even say that they are being cruelly expelled from the natural world. The very beings that ought to be the bearers of the new Christ revelation are being expelled and scattered. The Christ wants to approach the earth in the etheric realm, but He cannot be fully received. For in a dire response to His coming, elemental spirits are being driven away either entirely or partly from huge swathes of the earth, so that the enlivening effect of His proximity can only weakly reach the creatures and beings of the physical earth. And in contrast, from technological civilization and media proliferation, the immense armies of demonic elemental beings inimical to the human and the living world come simultaneously, dispatched into the earth's atmosphere like clouds of smoke to conceal what the light reveals.

This is how the most important spiritual event of our epoch is taking place. When, with the aid of our vessel of knowledge reverently raised we grasp the drama that is occurring, a fundamental attitude to the earth arises: of prime importance for us human beings is not the anxiety we feel about ecological damage, or the global risk to human health and human life, but something far more important than this: the tragic lack of acknowledgement of Christ's approach. Consequently, the most important goal of our ecological concern for nature should be to re-instate the elemental beings driven from their fields of activity and re-establish their rightful domains and realms of activity. And the fundamental stance of human beings who approach knowledge with reverence could be summed up as:

their longing to re-instate *an environment nurtured by elemental beings,* thus allowing the earth to be pervaded by undiminished light from the Christ sphere.

And what of the basic stance of soul in relation to humanity? Here, again, there is one thing of utmost importance for human beings in our time; and again it is Christ's reappearance. How should we witness and share in it? There are a number of ways of looking at it, one of which is more important than the others: the Christ, in His new manifestation, appears as 'karmic judge'; that is, as the one who assumes the task of putting human destinies in order. In doing so, He is bringing about more than cosmically just compensation for our human deeds; is doing more than providing opportunities for us to make redress to ourselves and our surroundings for the occasions, centuries ago, when we failed and were found wanting. Through sacrificing Himself, Christ became the bearer of all humanity's destiny. And He in now taking upon himself the redress of individual destinies, is harmonizing individual destinies with the overall destiny of humankind. The significance of the concepts of 'good' and 'evil' is changing; human beings can no longer be good only for themselves personally, without thinking of the wellbeing of humanity. What destiny brings to human beings, the strokes of destiny they suffer, should signify for them not only the possibility of advancement for themselves alone, but for the whole of humanity. From now on an individual's destiny is born out of humankind's overall karma.

If we contemplate this meditatively then our life of feeling will inevitably be imbued with a new sense of belonging to all humanity, a new awareness of responsibility not only for our own actions but also for what everyone else does.

(Perhaps this again is a characteristic feature of an 'anthroposophical image of the human being'?) Those who work to make anthroposophical knowledge their own by deepening it sufficiently will experience themselves as participating, in all humility, in humanity's common destiny, will feel something beyond concern merely for their own lives and for safeguarding their own future. Outer security no longer in fact exists; the whole of humanity has lost this. There is only spiritual security: the potential to collaborate with Christ on humanity's karma in an outwardly invisible way; or, to be more precise: the possibility of working faithfully on oneself so as to participate in Christ's ongoing sacrifice on behalf of humankind. The Christian martyrs and the great prophets of Christianity felt something similar, though not yet with an emphasis on sharing all humanity's common destiny. This is the new impetus that anthroposophy gives.

And so the fundamental stance of soul towards humanity, as anthroposophy conveys it, could be expressed as follows: *All that happens to humanity also happens to me. I share responsibility for all that happens, and will help bear the consequences, just as Christ continually helps us to bear all our burdens.*

Footnotes

GA (Gesamtausgabe) plus volume number refers to the Collected Works of Rudolf Steiner in German, published by the Rudolf Steiner Verlag, Dornach. Lecture dates, in the form of day/month/year, are given where appropriate.

1. *Foundations of Human Experience* (formerly published as *The Study of Man*), Lecture VIII, 29.8.1919, GA 293
2. *Human and Cosmic Thought*, GA 151
3. *The Theory of Knowledge Implicit in Goethe's World Conception* (1985)/*The Science of Knowing* (1988), Chapter 14: 'The Ground of Things and the Activity of Knowing', GA 2
4. *Occult Science – An Outline* (1969)/ *An Outline of Occult Science* (1972), Chapter 1: 'The Character of Occult Science', GA 13
5. GA 156, 19.12.1914 (Currently not available in English)
6. *Anthroposophical Leading Thoughts* (1973), 'Historic Cataclysms at the Dawn of the Spiritual Soul', 5.4.1925, GA 26
7. *The Story of My Life* (1928), Chapter 8, GA 28
8. *The Story of My Life* (1928), Chapter 7, GA 28
9. *The Theory of Knowledge Implicit in Goethe's World Conception* (1985)/*The Science of Knowing* (1988), GA 2, see footnotes to the German new edition of 1924
10. *The Threshold of the Spiritual World* (1922), Chapter 1: 'Concerning the Reliance which may be placed on Thinking; the Nature of the Thinking Soul; and of Meditation', GA17
11. For example, in *The Story of My Life* (1928), Chapters 8-10, GA 28
12. *The Human Soul in Relation to World Evolution*, 7.5.1922, GA 212
13. *The Story of My Life* (1928), Chapter 10, GA 28

14. *Occult Science – An Outline* (1969)/ *An Outline of Occult Science* (1972), Chapter 5: 'Cognition of the Higher Worlds – Initiation', GA 13
15. *Knowledge of the Higher Worlds*, Chapter 1: 'How is Knowledge of the Higher Worlds Attained?'/ 'Conditions', GA 10
16. Two characteristic examples: 'If our thinking is gradually to be brought more and more into order, to develop on the right lines so that our thoughts shall no longer be chaotic and confused, but filled, permeated with inner feeling, if there is to be an increasing development of healthy thinking based upon truth –
    '*Pre-Earthly Deeds of Christ*, 7.3.1914, Steiner Book Centre, Inc, 1976, GA 152
    'I would like first of all, very briefly, to examine the mood of soul needed by the spiritual researcher and also, to a certain extent, by anyone who would recognize the truth of the results of spiritual-scientific research... [He/She] must above all have an attitude of awe and unbounded reverence towards truth and knowledge.'
    Life Beyond Death, Chapter 1: 'Life Between Death and Rebirth', 19.3.1914, Rudolf Steiner Press, 1995, GA 63
17. *Karmic Relationships: Esoteric Studies - Volume III*, 28.7.1924, GA 237
18. *Anthroposophical Leading Thoughts* (1973), 'Michael's Mission in the Cosmic Age of Human Freedom', 16.11.1924, GA 26
19. *Anthroposophical Leading Thoughts* (1973), 'At the Dawn of the Michael Age', 17.08.1924, GA 26
20. *Practical Training in Thought*, 18.1.1909, GA 108
21. *Knowledge of the Higher Worlds*, Chapter 1: 'How is Knowledge of the Higher Worlds Attained?'/ 'Conditions', GA 10
22. *The Theory of Knowledge Implicit in Goethe's World Conception* (1985)/*The Science of Knowing* (1988), Chapter 13: 'The Activity of Knowing' and Chapter 14: 'The Ground of Things and the Activity of Knowing', GA 2
23. *The Story of My Life* (1928), Chapter 10, GA 28
24. *The Philosophy of Freedom*, Chapter 7: 'Are There Limits to Knowledge?', GA 4
25. *The Story of My Life* (1928), Chapter 7, GA 28

26. *The Theory of Knowledge Implicit in Goethe's World Conception* (1985)/*The Science of Knowing* (1988), see footnotes to the German new edition of 1924, GA 2
27. *Occult Science – An Outline* (1969)/ *An Outline of Occult Science* (1972), Chapter 1: 'The Character of Occult Science', GA 13
28. *Occult Science – An Outline* (1969)/ *An Outline of Occult Science* (1972), Chapter 1: 'The Character of Occult Science', GA 13
29. Particularly: *Karmic Relationships: Esoteric Studies – Volume IV*, 10.9.1924, GA 238
30. *Knowledge of the Higher Worlds*, Chapter 1: 'Inner Tranquillity', GA 10
31. *Anthroposophical Leading Thoughts* (1973), 'Michael's Mission in the Cosmic Age of Human Freedom', 16.11.1924, GA 26
32. *Theosophy*, Chapter 3, Section 5: 'The Physical World and its Connection with the Soul and Spiritland', GA 9
33. *Theosophy*, Chapter 3, Section 5: 'The Physical World and its Connection with the Soul and Spiritland', GA 9
34. *Goethean Science*, Chapter 1: 'Introduction', GA 1, (*Goethes Naturwissenschaftliche Schriften, Einleitungen*, Vol. IV, GA 1d)
35. *Death as Metamorphosis of Life*, 'How Do I Find the Christ?', 16.10.1918, GA 182
36. *Earthly Knowledge and Heavenly Wisdom*, 'Moral Impulses and Their Physical Manifestations: Taking Up a Spiritual Path', 18.2.1923, GA 221
37. *The Etherisation of the Blood*, 1.10.1911, GA 130,
38. *Awakening to Community*, 23.1.1923, GA 257
39. *Foundations of Human Experience* (formerly published as *The Study of Man*), Lecture IX: 30.8.1919, GA 293
40. *The Theory of Knowledge Implicit in Goethe's World Conception* (1985)/*The Science of Knowing* (1988), Chapter 16: 'Organic Nature', GA 2
41. Greater detail may be found, for example, in Thomas Göbel's *Die Pflanzenidee als Organon*. Niefern-Öschelbronn, 1988 (translation currently not available)
42. *Occult Science – An Outline* (1969)/ *An Outline of Occult Science* (1972), Chapter IV: 'The Evolution of the Cosmos and Man', GA 13

43. *The Challenge of the Times*, 7.12.1918 (quoted from the German 1921 first edition), GA 186
44. *The Social Question as a Problem of Soul Life*, 28.3.1919, GA 190
45. *Occult Science – An Outline* (1969)/ *An Outline of Occult Science* (1972), Chapter V: 'Cognition of the Higher Worlds – Initiation', GA 13
46. *Knowledge of the Higher Worlds*, Chapter 1: 'How is Knowledge of the Higher Worlds Attained?'/'Conditions', GA 10
47. *The World of the Senses and the World of the Spirit*, 27.12.1911, GA 134
48. *Occult Science – An Outline* (1969)/ *An Outline of Occult Science* (1972), Chapter IV: 'The Evolution of the Cosmos and Man', GA 13
49. *Man and the World of Stars and the Spiritual Communion of Mankind*, 31.12.1922, GA 219
50. *Anthroposophical Leading Thoughts* (1973), 17.2.1924, GA 26
51. *Man and the World of Stars and the Spiritual Communion of Mankind*, 31.12.1922, GA 219
52. *Man and the World of Stars and the Spiritual Communion of Mankind*, 31.12.1922, GA 219

The main sources for the publication of Rudolf Steiner's books and lectures in English are:
Rudolf Steiner Press www.rudolfsteinerpress.com
Steinerbooks www.steinerbooks.org
Mercury Press www.mercurypress.org